Astronauts Arrive in the Garden of Eden

Astronauts Arrive in the Garden of Eden

Haikus From Another Place

Billy Traylor

Names, characters, businesses, places, events and incidents are the products of the author. Any resemblance to actual persons, living or dead, or actual places or events is purely coincidental.

Printed in the United States of America
Wooden Pants Publishing
Fort Collins, Colorado
First Printing, 2018

ISBN: 10: 0-9992039-5-9
ISBN-13: 978-0-9992039-5-8

Cover image: Daniele Pietrobelli

DEDICATION

To Amanda, who is everything

Contents

A NOTE ON THE SYLLABLE COUNT

READ THESE POEMS IN YOUR BEST NORTH GEORGIA ACCENT SOME EXAMPLES ARE:

EVERY IS 2 SYLLABLES
SQUIRREL IS 1
ACTUALLY IS 3
FINALLY IS 2
HOUR IS 2
ESPECIALLY IS 3
RICHARD PRYOR IS 3
PROBABLY IS 2, BUT OCCASIONALLY 3
... AND SO FORTH

Act one: The Beginning

The sinister girl
delivers a birthday cake
to her friend's back door

Boy gets so nervous
telling jokes that his voice shakes
so, he fakes fainting

Pollock's Uncle Carl
continues the dripping style
but only does vans

Paul Klee for his kids
cuts a near impossible
Jack O' Lantern face

Each chorus member
has claves they click softly
to imply suspense

Ginger finds some brains
wrapped in palm leaves hidden in
the Professor's hut

Empty tortoise shell
now the site for some black ants'
Olympic style games

The zombie tiger
limps after us so slowly
we don't need to run

I
The kids think it's cool
when I drive in heavy rain
without wipers on

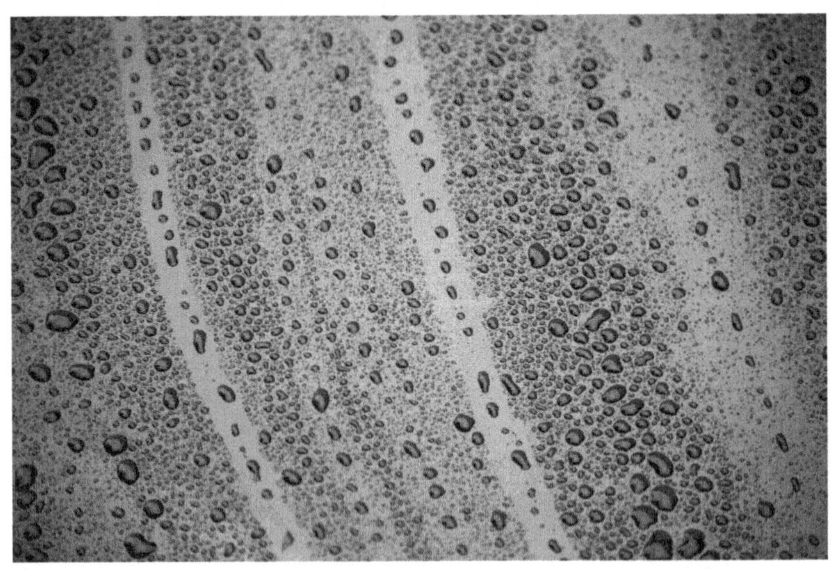

II
The secret to it
is you really concentrate
while leaning forward

The Little Richard
String Quartet performs Lucille
with much glissando

The cop refuses
to listen to my excuse
about the blood stain

Farmer Gustafsson
keeps rat snakes in his corn crib
FREE varmint control

The Memphisaurus
looked a bit like Elvis crossed
with some Gomer Pyle

P.O.W.
climbs the fence wearing armor
made from bent buckets

As he got older
his signature scribbled down
to a few smudges

Girl shows up at work
after having been out sick
with a new hairdo

The hit done flawless
By Kangaroo and Green Jeans
Mr. Moose accused

She sends me emails
only when she's mad at me
I still save them though

My four-year-old
drew horns on my passport photo
so, I got detained

Lizzie's school teacher
when she was late most mornings
"Where's that Borden girl?"

I fake a long throw
My dumb dog takes off running
Stops, looks back, forgives

Bought the game of Life
Chose the red car but crashed it
into the spinner

We're Parsley and Sage
I'm Sage, interpretive dance
She's Parsley, field drum

My father's old tools
wait patiently for projects
I probably won't start

Clearing out her house
we found Mom's baggie labeled
Lost Puzzle Pieces

High schooler in robes
strikes a cool pose in the fog
for his girlfriend's phone

Spelunking seamstress
discovered her spool of thread
was not long enough

I'd make the worst crook
because I can NOT control
the catch in my voice

Things to do today
1. water plants, 2. bend time,
3. watch cooking shows

Your shadow is sharp
Mine in contrast is fuzzy
thus matching my thoughts

Trillions of acorns
carpet the shady landscape
on the Oak's planet

Made of chicken wire
he easily walks through wind
Leaves are trouble though

The prudish girl's dreams
where she jumps out of a cake
bother her no end

Star field goal kicker
goes retro with no face mask
and wears bifocals

Shoes of the future
are wider because mankind
starts tipping over

Proof we've had visits
Photos of Neanderthals
found in a French cave

A fuzzy bee butt
sticks out of a flower bud
that's not quite open

On the hairpin turn
my sports car loses its brakes
and I Knievel

Dragstrip hussy fruges
with a klutz in a crew cut
and a cream blazer

Pagan paints giant
bloodshot eyeball on his shield
Drinks mead while it dries

I love belly rubs
I purr and go all dreamy
then lash out scratchin'

The cook was murdered
in the crab shack parking lot
between two Buicks

Watch the giraffe sneeze
It's nose almost bangs the ground
and it whips up dust

The best kinds of crunch
Macadamias followed
closely by crushed ice

Square white guy plays sax
Sounds as square as square can be
I'm not kidding, square

First soul in Heaven
lonely for just a moment
until Two shows up

Scratchy transmission
seems otherworldly to me
and my Ham buddies

His brass belt buckle
left in the blob creature's wake
His fillings also

My pet hummingbird
likes SweeTarts dissolved in Sprite
You talk about zip

Zoo's camel sees rain
Knows exactly what to do
Mopes back to the shed

She waters a plant
with bland tea Ted made for her
once he's left the room

Found at the crime scene
Plastic card of Xanax pills
with a few punched out

Old Martin guitar
A worn hole near the pickguard
he's mighty proud of

All-consuming itch
from cut hairs down his collar
while he robs the bank

Act Two: We Have Landed

Astronauts arrive
in the Garden of Eden
to trap that serpent

North Korean hacks
took over the Pentagon
and Reader's Digest

Mouse safely watches
it's friend in the cage trap eat
maybe it's last cheese

I treasured that cloud
from Live Peace in Toronto
1969

Real attractive girl
except she grins like E.T.
which sets me aback

I don't dig a ditch
unless I absolutely
HAVE to dig a ditch

Miles Davis' tone
As much to do with slouching
as it did with mutes

The heaviest soul
Weighed 4 pounds 7 ounces
Most weigh 6 ounces

When I fall I think
of friends I've not kept up with
as I'm going down

Outlaw Yule Brynner
just kept coming and coming
even with no face

Doug Flutie rares back
and unleashes one downfield then
dodges a late hit

The girl dragonfly
fakes death to avoid meeting
suitors she dislikes
(They really do that)

A clowder of cats
A plethora of problems
A poog of haystacks

Cat has a birdhouse
for a head, so for supper
just sits quietly

Ant, ant, ant, ant, ant,
ant, ant, ant, ant with leaf, ant,
ant, ant, ant, ant, ant

She points, goes "Baaah-am!"
that's a two syllable bam
It's become her thing

Love my Saturn hat
except the rings keep falling down
onto my shoulders

I've not had goosebumps
since I saw Uncle Clem's ghost
10 Easters ago

"Pointy green gas cans"
That's what they call palmettos
when there's a wild fire

I have the power
to see into the future
I don't see you though

My B-17
I would name THE KITCHEN SINK
and drop my bombs last

Bold entrepreneur
scoops up Boston Harbor tea
Sells it as keepsakes

Red, yellow, and blue
were on sale so Mondrian
bought those, and left green

Rain slowly soaks down
Softens my cheap coffin lid
until it buckles

One wind molecule
grinding against another
Sound of a freight train

Bee sting flavored chips
So hot they intimidate
scotch bonnet people

Raccoon learns to talk
Can say "fish", "let's go fishing",
and "squeeze of lemon"

Boss comes up to me
"Trim your nails on your own time"
So, 2 short 3 long

Sahara Batman
prowls the sand dunes fully caped
Leaves deep round footprints

New Orleans jazz band
Their sign: REQUESTS $5
"SAINTS" $15

Scorpion stumbles
running over a pebble
and face plants the sand

She's pro mosquito
and moved to Siberia
where there are trillions

Napoleon dies
The death mask maker stands by
with plasters and creams

Joe Namath scolded
for having his cowboy boots
up on the sofa

Einstein loved ping pong
and could produce so much spin
the balls arched sideways

Triplets walk the mall
in step, turning together
like a school of fish

Sniffer dog sniffs socks
worn by dementia patients
who've wandered away

Soy sauce bottle
dropped, bounces, but doesn't break
Soy sauce gets crema

2041
A lightning strike starts brush fires
in Antarctica

Prank sized Elmer's Glue
in the white gallon jug
waits for the right idea

I'm surely having
the Yahtzee game of my life
Planets might align

Even in his grave
his tomb stone's struck by lightning
like he was 3 times

Mom serves canned pear halves
with mounds of Miracle Whip
dolloped on each one

My Lego eclipse
done in black and yellow blocks
Corona's yellow

Perilous drill bit
comes spiraling through the wall
from the work next door

Kids in Kyoto
leave coins for the bullet train
to smash atom flat

I take good Advice
from a 200-year-old
koi named Butterfly

Interstate 80
on the way to Burning Man
Huge towed harlequin

Wasabi nachos
with kumquat/kiwi salad
then licorice pudding

One publishing house
sent back an email with link
"How to Write Haikus"

Dropped my chili fries
on our new Berber carpet
Then did the whole room

He's angry, riled, stressed
His dog won't come when he calls
Yep, that dog is wise

The deaf signing guy
overdoing storm warnings
is star of the show

The intrepid mutt
with ammo in his backpack
for pinned down soldiers

control alt delete
“Come on!!”, control alt delete
“What’s wrong with this thing!!”

Act Three: The Future

2025
My tetanus shot's a gummy
and cola flavored

10-year-old dollop
of apricot jam dried hard
like Russian amber

Benevolent troll
tries briefly to calm the goat
dragged under the bridge

Neptune stands in the surf
glaring at the beach while waves
splash him in the back

Model employee
keeps pulling up mahjong games
but x-ing right out

Ringo Starr at bat
Floats a looping fly to left
Yoko misjudges

I'm joining a cult
It's a good way to find friends
who will stay stay stay

Planet Earth explodes
Eons later passing probes
find a cheese grater

I'll test that jet pack
I need some smokes and'll have
one on the way back

Unsuspecting toads
end up with wished away warts
not birthday wishes

I coughed while I yawned
and made a loud hahg hahg sound
moistening my eyes

Navy jet lands hard
Skids off the deck and dangles
by its cable hook

Tripped, fell forward, flipped
Landed on my feet, yelled "Yeah!!"
Can't brag, no one saw

Grandpa's best scarecrow
was a big fox looking thing
toting a shotgun

Fierce river people
stare hard at us from the bank
then pull out blowguns

Bear pushes its head
through our cat door and gets stuck
Our kid feeds it grapes

Don't understand it
Therefore, I like it a lot
Will you take a check?

Offered a raccoon
my smore, which it took, then stole
all my marshmallows

Saxophone player
who does circular breathing
hogs the arrangements

Sitting on the curb
having a smoke in drizzle
behind Waffle House

Ferdinand the roach
crushed to death by a house shoe
Friends speak of great loss

Posing in the yard
in her Easter dress, white gloves
holding a pitchfork

iPhone etiquette
Don't say "Check out these pictures"
and hand it to them

Path of the bullet
takes it across the dark room
out the open door

My art makes you mad
and, you know, that's exactly
what I'm going for

Yves Klein thought up blue
then had a few second thoughts
but just WENT with it

The bank repossessed
my wonderful pile of wood
while I financed nails

Cat hair dust bunny
looks just like a lost angel
under our bunk beds

"Smells like fried okra
in here just a little bit"
he said to the Monk

I sculpt girls in veils
You can just make out the face
if you give it time

Our missile flies low
disturbing uppermost leaves
of uncaring oaks

Anchor swing set legs
to the ground with concrete
if your kid swings hard

Dizzy octopus
lives in a sunken soup can
that rolls with the tides

Family photograph
Charlie Duke left on the Moon
with welcoming smiles

Forgotten scarecrows
endure the Nebraska snow
on their outstretched arms

Still make ginger bread
and pressure cooker green beans
cooked down to a mush

I swatted a fly
that was so huge I'll need to
bury the body

English pantomime
The kids yell "He's behind you !!"
but he doesn't look

Butterfly caught out
in heavy rain hides in our
empty bird feeder

Bear grass monkey grass
A bear might call it monkey
and a monkey bear

Small door in a tree
with a nice beveled window
and porcelain knob

Ghost in a rowboat
at the Battle of the Nile
barely got noticed

I thought I heard birds
chirping at night, but it was
just my nose whistling

It's Chesterfield Brown
Newest color by Glidden
Ideal for most barns

Ornate tapestry
of an old-fashioned comet
hangs at the villa

"History of the Frown"
an unusual essay
for a clown to write

Binocular club
meets Wednesday mornings on that
mountain over there

One small brown leaf
from the old oak overhead
floating in my tea

Napoleon kept
a bad smell map of Egypt
and was a huge creep

A bag of balloons
kept in my desk at work
We forget birthdays

Try levitation
if you're falling down the stairs
Really concentrate

Shadowy figure
at the top of our back yard
Watching, motionless

A distant siren
An ambulance on the move
Train horn chimes in too

Robots take over
when the astronauts leave
the crippled spaceship

Coming through the trees
gentle winds aid the long march
of the leaf army

Dance like a chicken
Arch your back, put hands on hips
do a nice head bob

Planet Krispy Kreme
Its moon shaped like a doughnut
and seas coffee black

Cold beyond compare
and no breathtaking colors
Sunset on Pluto

A coloring book
each page colored solid black
by the young patient

Shaken up, flying
on a broom over rooftops
Salem witch snow globe

We're missing ponies
They were tied up near Loch Ness
What could have happened?

Act Four: Burnt Toast Eden

Grandpa burns the toast
Grandma has a hissy fit
and threatens Grandpa

Swell of the ocean
Dark of the rain forest floor
Sweep of the big sky

A crawlspace angel
Not the first place you'd expect
an angel to be

Valdosta chipmunks
have a plan for a tunnel
to Miami Beach

It's been gone a while
THE END at the end of films
Gone like the caboose

A strong rascal wind
blows all our neighbor's pine cones
into our front yard.

The brash killer whales
swim up very close to shore
Don't walk in the surf

A hungry Sasquatch
walks up to my car window
and taps on the glass

Loud screechy vocals
Flailing a ukulele
Sister on drum set

A huge monster bat
forgotten by history
terrorized Roanoke

Song stuck in your head?
Hum "It's Not Unusual"
to clear it quickly

Portrait of a duck
It's a relative of mine
See, I'm a duck too

Faint sounds from the lab
High pitched buzzing and chirping
from Moon rocks on shelves

Aliens attack
Dirt clods rain down from above
They're from a dirt world

Continental drift
Baha heads to Alaska
but taking it's time

Night's almost arrived
Everything's dark but tree tops
that shine the last light

My favorite puddle
You splash through it with your car
Does a nice low spray

I'm an indoor mouse
Don't coax me out in the sun
I'm an indoor mouse

Long smears of dark green
across a field of light green
I've strolled through the dew

Very tough barn cat
keeps the mice under control
That cat's Popeye tough

One of the great tools
we have at our disposal
Our wondrous thumbnail

The half rock creature
can't climb into our tree house
so, I think we're safe

Cola will melt nails
and take road grime off bumpers
Good with popcorn too

Pygmies have a song
for honey gathering and
hunting with a net

Our Spitfire fighters
use their wings to flip V-1's
that putter along

Lewis Carroll's cat
pushes cards off the table
into a top hat

Sea monster drawings
created by Magellan
Still useful today

Graves on the island
badly marked and littered with
fallen coconuts

Don't throw them at things
or get cuts or run with them
rockpaperscissors

There's a hidden chip
in the binding of each one
Catcher in the Rye

Disappearing ink
Accidentally used it
on my tax return

A being from space
Not flesh and bone, made of wood
with sticky sap blood

I was only three
couldn't resist the cactus
and grabbed it just once

Bereft of ideas
I stare at the blank blank page
You see what I mean?

Tree falls silently
Sound needs an ear to be heard
No ear was around

When I make curry
I think "Thai fishing village"
and pretend I'm there

Here's a little hint
A Bullwinkle coffee mug
would make a great gift

Amanda's WYVERN
played on the triple word space
ruined Scrabble for me

I erase a lot
and daydream one day I could
erase decisions

Weed covered frogmen
splashing out of the lagoon
Gilligan's concerned

Monkey and weasel
Monkey does the swing set best
Weasel does the slide

Dream HO scale train
would have two freight train engines
pulling just flatcars

Watercolors bleed
The hill merges with the sky
because you rushed it

Three Crabs fish sauce wins
The most beautiful label
of all the labels

THE DAY DREAMING PIG
HAS ABSOLUTELY NO TEXT
IN IT'S THOUGHT BUBBLE

RINSE AND THEN REPEAT?
DON'T!! THEY JUST WANT YOU TO BUY
MORE OF THEIR SHAMPOO

TARZAN'S SON BOY
FLOATS ON A HUGE LILY PAD
SMOKING BETWEEN TAKES

THOSE STRIP MINE DUMP TRUCKS
HAVE A MILLION-DOLLAR TRUCK
JUST TO CHANGE THEIR TIRES

SOME WELL-KNOWN RED THINGS:
BLOOD, MARS, STOP SIGNS, RIPE PEPPERS
AND GRAND FUNK'S SECOND

To treat the Black Death
A warm poultice of butter,
onion, and garlic

Huge clap of thunder
startles the wedding party
Then the lights go out

The vagabond child
hiding in the library
near the travel books

Headhunter haircut
Beads, braids, highlights made from blood
Hard do to maintain

The toy jet takes off
from the kitchen countertop
Destination, the den

Dolls on the sofa
sit there like they own the place
They probably do

Hypnotist was lame
We left feeling constantly
stuck in whirlpools, though

Thought the red-faced guy
may have has Tourette's, but no
He just cussed a lot

Dodge City's peaceful
ever since the stagecoach brought
the rhinoceros

Tchaikovsky's winter
A dull sun behind bare trees
in a minor key

Act Five: Vegetarian Crocodiles

Rub your finger on glass
fast, like you're removing spots
Goes queeka queeka

Low pulsating hum
Cargo ship's diesel engines
idling in port

The board game couple
always makes us play Sorry
when we visit them

Sent to the Air Force
One thousand "TOP SECRET" stamps
Block letters, red ink

New knitting project
A hot water bottle cozy
before my next ache

DEW line in Greenland
watched for Soviet bombers
stocked vodka and gin

Gnats, late afternoon
spinning around each other
in a beam of light

"Arctic Summer Poem"
cold cold cold cold cold warm cold
cold cold cold cold cold

Gigantic snowball
screaming down the hill with feet
stuck out wearing skis

Millions of leaves fall
I can make piles all day long
I'm built for raking

Burning red hot bright
The tiles on the space shuttle
stubborn to get home

Zulu beer basket
When it's wet it's water tight
for the family brew

Surprised a T-Rex
on the Appalachian trail
near the Georgia line

Ghost notes on drum set
Soft sounds struck between loud ones
You hear them, but don't

Plethora of koi
jostling up near the surface
where we have pellets

The river rises
Water laps against the door
A little gets in

I love bulgogi
so much so I'm always sad
when the meal's over

The Mary Rose sinks
Cannons point toward the sky
as she rolls over

The curtain won't close
and the machine eats the card
Voting booth 13

Childhood switch goes off
Suddenly you like mustard
Years on, black coffee

Magnet on a chain
With 10,000 staples stuck
Pulled from paper sludge

Dogs' and cats' dew claws
Both try to evolve a thumb
That'll be the day

The age-old problem
Homemade cookies dropping crumbs
Eat them upside down

I
My friend's model tanks
looked like they'd been in action
then parked in the woods

II
Glue oozed out of seams
Fingerprints in the gloss paint
That's what mine looked like

The judgmental man
glares at our tall grass unmowed
while he walks his dog

I don't get skeeter bit
or itch from poison ivy
Bothered by gnats though

Pacing back and forth
wringing my hands because cops
are at the front door

Hid in the bushes
outside ballroom dancing class
instead of going

"Sex in the City"
preferred by ISIS fighters
resting back at camp

The Unabomber
drops by the Minute Market
for a grape Icee

What you can not buy
A voice, a knack, a true friend,
the Moon, and that yacht

Needlepoint troll
scary, framed, hung in the hall
Oh yeah, it's life-size

Chimney sweep legend
Square Bob was stuck for 8 days
Lived on rain water

Smashed eggs on the ground
Mother bird's long flown off
Some cat's had a feast

Kangaroo babies
bouncing all over the place
in a cloud of dust

The Mayan gift shop
has End of Days calendars
at closeout pieces

Wood ages and dries
Driven nails once tight, loosen
and fall to the ground

Pinpoint sized worm holes
Our parallel universe
gets cat hair and lint

The lost mariner
adrift on the open sea
lays down in his boat

The click of checkers
jumping others intrigues me
more than winning games

Zen Garden murder
Constables trample the scene
Ruin the sand patterns

Matisse's suitcase
An old fiberboard model
Full of paint stained pants

A phantom chair floats
out one house, across the yard,
into the next house

Buzzards on the road
convene around something new
A melting Heath bar

The Shut-Up Fairy
You start saying anything
it'll shut you down

Fake vomit, fake poop,
squirting flower, cayenne gum,
hand buzzer, no friends

Added rope seatbelts
Old pickup's still not safe though
Needs burlap air bags

Tense praying mantis
clinging to a skyscraper
Each step still upwards

Christo's Christmas gifts
Unwrap them Christmas morning
and ruin their value

Looking all mellow
dolphins in a dumb painting
gaze up at the Moon

Candy Apple Jones
Custom painted cars and boats
Known for her reds

Guy I know's hobby's
visiting all courthouses
in every county

Fly flies toward him
He snatches it in mid air
and wads it up dead

Winnebago stops
right at the edge of the cliff
One tire hangs over

Act Six: Orange Astronaut Knocking

I

Experimental
sheet music with instructions
"Don't play this, hide it"

II

And in a few years
someone else finds it, reads it,
and hides it again

Rogue kamikaze
his cockpit radio tuned
to big band music

Knock knock. Who's there? Orange
Orange who? Orange you glad haikus
don't do knock knock jokes.

Sometimes you may think
you want fish, but in fact you
just want tartar sauce

Bought a new album
by a cabaret singer
named FiFi LaFemme

Cow mimics whale song
Amazes all the farmers
Farm bureau men too

Cambodian soup
Spiced coconut milk, chicken,
and a glaze of fat

Sleeping bear totem
Not pole shaped, it's boulder shaped
Depicts stored up strength

Use your bike to pull
that wagon full of hay bales
Take the pitchfork, too

Step to start long hike
Nail to start building a shed
Match to start fire dance

Laying in a field
Parachute didn't open
Could be here some time

Don't moisten your thumb
to pick up spilled hole punch dots
Use rolled up Scotch tape

Bikini Atoll
coconuts and radishes
still aren't safe to eat

Why do most cowboys
push their hats back on their heads
when they're pondering?

Campbells soup colors
inspired by the uniforms
of Cornell football

I

Serial killer
in Japan leaves haiku poems
behind as a clue

II

One crime scene haiku
makes investigators gaze
briefly at the clouds

Rendering in clay
of the Hindenburg crashing
Blimp's good but flames aren't

Kids have cereal
Watch Indian test patterns
until cartoons start

Dick Van Dyke's rare skill
Backwards sentence any say
instantly can he

Wind reshapes the dunes
Wisps of sand blown up the sides
disperse in the air

Solid gray painting
Color applied with sponges
Texture of the Moon

A baby spider's
first attempt at traveling
on a single strand

Sandbars of sugar
wait in my cereal bowl
for me to dredge down

A paper cup floats
down the river to the sea
What was in it, gone

Your smile's beautiful
and your laugh's music to me
Your nod's even good

Her Chatty Cathy
stopped chatting after it got
it's first bubble bath

Phone's about to ring!!
I can just sense it, really
Wait for it... Wait... Wait...

Giant wears a house
he's yanked up from the village
Wears it like a hat

Zulu warriors
use stolen rifles to shoot
into the compound

She gives a side-eye
to the widow at the bar
in a low-cut blouse

Tired trick or treaters
have enough candy for months
Just want to be done

The Cardiff giant
Hoax revealed by the sculptor
who was never paid

Lots more Stone Mountains
buried under the surface
all across the South

"Beach Piece"
Yell at gulls -- throw sand
1969 autumn
by Yoko Ono

Toys from Cracker Jacks
Biggest collection in fact
is in Pontiac

Slowly and red hot
Lava surrounds a Stop sign
Makes it redundant

Two rabbits boxing
both up on their hind legs lit
by our Jeep's headlights

How to split seconds:
Chop them in half, lose one half,
Halve the other half

Serve Turkish coffee
Remind your guests that the silt
might ruin the last sip

We pay homage to
Princess Mohair and her son,
Prince Sonnyandcher

Whales and giraffes sleep
Whales just under the surface
Giraffes folded up

Clem walks furtively
away from the tractor wreck
he caused in the field

Describe hominy
"Think of it like if popcorn
was a vegetable"

Kind of expensive
Cheese rolled in volcanic ash
labeled Pompeiian

Missed all the comets
Never saw the Northern Lights
or had rhubarb pie

Had one lump of coal
so, my snowman's a cyclops
Had a carrot though

Ridges on toenails
Undiagnosed health problems?
or just some ridges

Careless night watchman
naps, doesn't check doors, leaves gun
on the loading dock

Documentary
about fonts, how they evolved,
and how they've changed us

Tiny tornado
blows the pink Jeep off the road
Kills Barbie and Ken

Pets don't understand
when you show them the red card
They should leave, but don't

Magician's bunny
smokes out back in the alley
until he goes on

She rests on boulders
glaciers brought eons ago
and left near the trail

Have yerba matte
on the side of Everest
in your lucky gourd

Trek through the desert
Someone hands you an Icee
and there's your brain freeze

Act Seven: Moon Pie Funeral

General Sherman
left hundreds of charred chimneys
all across Georgia

Used Corvair for sale
Be sure to check underneath
for puddles of oil

Fire truck custom paint
Either orange and yellow flames
or water splashing

Bent funeral fan
Kid played with it, fanned too hard
Not a good keepsake

Dad brought Moon Pies home
from the mill's vending machine
He thought I liked them

Dust rises up, chokes
Wind moves trash around, clutters
Rain falls down, cleans up

Huck Finn's raft floats by
Calm Mississippi evening
Jim's got his feet up

Other worldly green
like the Ford Gremlins of old
makes awful house paint

Mom says, "Clean your room"
with no please or pretty please
She's a bit fed up

Small blobs of fresh air
wait in the vastness of space
like skinless balloons

A disappointing meal
Pedestrian noodle dish
with walk away sauce

Brave girl, bow in hair,
tells the monster to stand still
Lines up an arrow

Picard's great white whale
The Crystalline Entity
just leveled the place

Like in a cartoon
I step on the hoe blade, whack!!
Handle smacks my nose

I watch Jeopardy
and so influenced by it
I speak in questions

Hunting giant sloths
men with spears crouch near bushes
all holding their breath

Man with plastic glove
picks up dog poop on their walk
Dog stands there, blank look

Bad dream from childhood
Angry ostriches surround
and peck at our car

Hollering contest
Judges are two miles away
One's a little deaf

Take the mountain quiz
It may even include caves
Win a rock hammer

A dozen oysters
on a cool platter of ice,
lemon, bit of grit

Greenish meteor
made mainly of emeralds
hits the poor man's shack

In the mushy swamp
strange lights are seen from the road
More and more cars stop

Nice custom inlay
on my Gibson guitar neck
Butter bean with sprout

Whiskers of a cat
used to scope out tight spaces
before they go in

"New $10 bills
look like they've been dropped in mud,"
said Mom with a frown

Angry hornet stung
my button pushing finger
I kept spraying though

Tough guys at my school
stuck tacks in their loafers' heels
to click "attitude"

Somali pirate
could have been the next Einstein
if he'd gone to school

Wiped up the syrup
with the sleeve of my sports coat
That was a mistake

When I see bacon
I think "How much can I eat
without being rude"

Lightnings flash the clouds
Thunders boom the countryside
Torrents rain the night

Stream near the tar pits
has its rainbow hue scattered
by a rock we threw

Leaves float on the pond
Fish gaze through them from below
at the trees above

Car full of bodies
at the bottom of the lake
not found for decades

Know your columns quiz
Corinthian, Dorian,
and Ionian

Turtle owns a kite
Doesn't play with it much though
Tends to just drag it

Erasers improved
They used to scratch it away
Now they smooth it gone

Was that thunder? No,
just the daily explosion
at the rock quarry

Car jumps out at you
and no one's behind the wheel
It's just a mean car

Visualizing
games of Spider Solitaire
helps me get to sleep

Brand new red Bobcat
won't get scratched up or muddy
Loads packing peanuts

We're leaving because
bullets rolled off the table
and down the heat vent

Smashed toes and crying
Children's' rock stacking party
was not a success

Don't know Cousin It
We didn't get that channel
Know Hoss Cartwright though

New lake floods the town
A half-submerged church steeple
All that's seen from shore

Paul Barnes drank a quart
of cold chocolate milk before
marching band practice

Basho dreamt haiku
Seldom woke to paint them down
so many were lost

Philip Guston's car
Pink, cloddish, in his late style
Yep, it's my dream car

The best back windshield
The Plymouth Barracuda
1966

Inner ear problem
keeps you veering to the left
as you're walking home

My nail halfway nailed
Bent, and there's dents all around
Dad says "Pitiful"

Aliens arrive
Concerned Earth's full of beings
that eat each other

GAVE MY LAVA LAMP
AWAY TO SOMEONE WHO WON'T
APPRECIATE IT

BLASTS FROM VOLLEY GUNS
CLEAR THE DECKS OF THE FRIGATE
WE'VE PULLED UP NEXT TO

WHAT WIND REALLY THINKS
BLOWING LEAVES IS A PLEASURE
SO'S WHIPPING UP FIRES

A MAN MADE OF STRAW
WALKS DOWN THE TRAIL WHILE BIRDS
STEAL BITS FOR THEIR NESTS

SERVED CHILI TO FRIENDS
GARNISHED WITH FREEZE DRIED RED ANTS
THEY GOT UP AND LEFT

Act Eight: Haiku Goalkeepers

The high tide reaches
her paperback on the beach
while she takes a nap

She reads my haiku
She laughs some thinking laughter
while she plans edits

The best goalkeepers
can see just a few seconds
into the future

All colors combined
should make black, but instead make
dark greenish purple

Clowns show up with rakes
to clear oak leaves that have blown
under the big top

Farm girl discovers
sticky spots left by the ghost
from the sorghum mill

Cat jumps on the sill
an upside-down squirrel falls hard
from the bird feeder

Moth's trip disrupted
There's a bright hundred-watt bulb
over our back door

The recluse studies
the ritual of hello
and handshakes as well

Paper hat sailboat
attacked by paper airplanes
with paper clip bombs

Meet the Rat family
Not rats, they're human beings
Their last name's just Rat

Art you just (boom) see
Music on the other hand
takes time to (booooooooooom) hear

Adoring patron
stands gazing at the Rothko
for like three hours

Never's dawned on cats
Instead of pulling straight back
Unhook from a snag

Wall of noise CD
Put it on at low volume
Get some thinking done

Old Faithful geyser
pranked by some geologists
with red dye and Joy

I

Charles sat on the edge
of our 14-story dorm
Dangled his legs off

II

To this very day
I still worry about Charles
doing that dumb stunt

"Hot diggity dog,"
was first said by Al Jolson
1928

Deep fried cantaloupe
instead of deep fried pork rinds
Big hit with vegans

Big storm coming in
Dogs hide, birds have stopped chirping,
the air seems thicker

I'm really hungry
that dizzy kind of hungry
A bit grouchy too

2 AM poolside
Bats skim the surface drinking
with their outstretched tongues

Chandelier comes loose
Crashes to the floor with a
BAM tinkle tinkle

Cat signals to me
"Billy, get down low like me
and we'll catch that bird"

Goldfish might like toys
Maybe some fishing line floats
to bump back and forth

I stepped on a bee
in the Congo, African,
the most dangerous

To avoid sand spurs
Dog tiptoes across the yard
with quite the stern look

Heard for miles around
The shrill call of the Wildman
and his pet blue jay

Face of the liar
Actually, many faces
That's how it's best done

Deer gather at dusk
to mess around eating grass
and share some ideas

Parking lot's so full
it looks like Woodstock out there
you know, where they parked

Lucky eels and crabs
find sunken Japanese tanks
and make them their home

Einstein mistaken
for a groundskeeper on break
He kind of liked that

Johnny Dandelion
unlike his Appleseed kin
never got much press

Fallen leaf in Fall
welcomed by those on the ground
and quickly fits in

First soak the decals
When they loosen glide then on
Then blot with tissue

My coyote friend
Front yard, sure, back yard no way
Cat's back there sunning

I

Papa had a cow
that was frightened of the lines
Wouldn't cross the road

II

so, he'd shovel dirt
on those white and yellow lines
and the cow did fine

Peace symbol sticker
Appalachian Trail decal
They're quite sierra

Pop you know what pop
pop pop I love pop pop pop
pop bubble wrap pop

Thought the doorbell rang
about 4 in the morning
I'm in bed, wide eyed

Palm reader predicts,
"Long life, good health, your team wins,
twenty dollars please"

Bird with a pebble
Drops it with head snap on cats
passing by below

Japanese Noh fan
helps move a little cool air
under that stiff mask

Bluebird feeds it's young
Starts strong but a few weeks on
gets a bit frazzled

Oooo!! rocket's red glare
Ahhh!! the bombs bursting in air
"Whew" proof through the night

Pipe organ improv
Tenor sax accompaniment
Sounds mighty Gothic

"It's the brand-new thing
everyone's talking about"
is sometimes a con

Claimed "Creek water's great"
so, he filled up his canteen
Sick later that night

It chased after me
that mean dog of the preacher's
like I was sinful

Spiked caterpillar
just moseys around the shrubs
No worries at all

Beyond the barbed wire
a much more interesting world
Or so the bull thought

Mourning dove eats snails
Sets one aside for its spouse
They're monogamous

Ms. Day wants Bee
as her new baby's first name
Mr. Day says "Think"

Act Nine: Carrot Crunch

Mouse glimpses itself
in the side of the toaster
Falls madly in love

Furrows level out
Farm house slowly falls to ruin
Windmill chokes with rust

Horse crunches carrots
gazing ahead at nothing
Blinks a fly away

Tacked up Lost Cat signs
Found her a few days later
at the fish 'n' chips.

Deleaf trees in a day
Have snow fall in one big lump
Hurry the Spring thaw

Postcard about toast
Stamp's from the butter series,
the one with the churn

The kid's a phenom
at sidewalk marble shooting
with his scooped-out thumb

Advanced monkey tribe
makes clothes out of vines and leaves
Even makes luggage

She tends her bonsai
She's patient and 93
They're not quite ready

Parking lot yard sale
Kids hide from the blazing sun
under the tables

Shadow of Hendrix
on the front of Marshall amps
Upside down headstock

Urgent Captain STOP
3 rescue ships en route STOP
6 hours out STOP

Went to the movies
in my corduroy house shoes
Saw "The Longest Day"

Magnolia leaf falls
turns brown, then takes like 10 years
to disintegrate

Found the Lost Dutchman
in the harsh Superstitions
guarded by rattlers

Westminster winner
Kit Carson, top chihuahua
Takes on all comers

An empty canoe
floats lonely down the river
toward the rapids

Lax time traveler
forgets to take off his watch
during the Bronze Age

Short guy wears striped shirt
Thinks it makes him look taller
so, he's got dozens

She saves the hour
when time changes in the Fall
to use when she's late

His car is covered
in a thick weave of pine straw
Not been cranked for months

I'm startled awake
by a wolf howling nearby
plus, my tent collapsed

Becky makes a doll
a tense looking voodoo doll
looks like her teacher

Clear lump on the beach
Remains of a jellyfish
sniffed by a poodle

Bought my frog gigger
to pick up magnolia leaves
that litter my yard

Angel ice fishes
All nibbles snatched through the hole
Angel's good at it

Mirror is honest
Shows the kindness in your eyes
and your bad hair day

Old chipped coffee cup
Rumored Elvis sipped from it
Goes big at auction

Sun shines on a stump
Doesn't do a bit of good
It remains a stump

Orange Fiestaware
could make leftover chili
radioactive

Newest LEDs
make a warmer yellow light
Dark's still the same though

Worst pillows ever
The Japanese block of wood
and the Vulcan tripod

Man carries his son
A toddler dressed just like him
Looks just like him too

When you get possessed
throw yourself out a window
That should do the trick

Grease some Vaseline
on fresh cut stubs of pruned shrubs
They sprout back faster

"Goodbye," says the book
"I've enjoyed our bent bindings
and dogeared corners"

My coat is on fire
Most times I'd just take it off
but my zipper's stuck

Going to supper
at the mushroom hunter's house
Little bit wary

New Guinea mudmen
in their grey clay pot shaped masks
with the angry eyes

In the waiting room
Man with an enormous foot
There for a nagging cough

Lonely place to wait
Soviet roadside bus stop
Tarza, Kazakhstan

Get good at chopsticks
Practice picking up marbles
and steering your car

Took home some wood shards
from a tree struck by lightning
in case they're good luck

Blue ribbon winner
Origami soccer goal
complete with netting

Find me a new heart
One that takes much better care
of the ones I love

Iceberg near Haiti
Much photographed from the shore
Refuses to melt

Bumped into a bee
while riding a dragonfly
Fell off into moss

Slouching boy at church
looks down at his feet and sighs
then up to Heaven

Dents in the carpet
where chairs have been are foxholes
for my army men

"Flash", along with "Pop"
Neighborhood transformer blows
Out go all our lights

Man made of balloons
drinks iced tea, gets top heavy
as his head fills up

I walk on the beach
mimicking a camel's stride
Shoes still fill with sand

Whale craves rain water
Spends more time near the surface
looking for dark clouds

Want bacon and eggs?
Chicken goes "yeah, no problem"
Pig takes off runnin'

Launch code for our nukes
was OOOOOO...
for like twenty years!

Huh? transcends language
Understood by everyone
in the entire world

Small holes in the yard
where squirrels have dug for moisture
during the long drought

Spin the orrery
One planet falls off its mount
and dents on the floor

Rabbit's foot key chain's
got my car keys and house key
No flats or break-ins

Act Ten: Yankee Friends

Kids in the bait shop
knocked over the cricket cage
while they horsed around

Zigging and zagging
The Albatross is pursued
by Sopwith Camels

I tell Yankee friends
"No dog will sleep near kudzu,
it grows so damn fast"

Kid on Santa's lap
says he wants a tank of gas
like the dentists use

Trust your sushi chef
So what if your lips get numb
from his puffer fish

Leaf against the curb
held there by some steady wind
Brown and upside down

My best souvenir
A tumbleweed from out west
Keep it in the den

For a split second
two planes colliding head on
will touch nose to nose

General Sherman
shook hands with slaves as he marched
toward Savannah

Discarded umbrella
The brella part was ok
but the um's broken

Orange juice hates coffee
Sip one then sip the other
one time you'll agree

With Roman candles
I'm an extremely good shot
With dirt clods as well

Sunlight strikes the web
Bright lines shine then disappear
in wind at sunset

Floaters in my eyes
follow in their own slow gait
quick glances I make

Found a butcher knife
in the woods near the train tracks
Might be some hobo's

My flying carpet
resides flat in the alcove
until I call it

Flowers grow in Hell
Asbestos blooms, poisonous,
and hard on the eyes

Bridge anxiety
When I hit that metal grate
I feel a slight swerve

I care for sick friends,
get sympathetic symptoms
and drop by Walgreen's

Back from Vietnam
he'd jump behind the sofa
at any loud noise

I sit with Gary
at the edge of the corn field
while he shoots at crows

World War I London
Grey zeppelins crawl the night sky
lit by searchlight beams

From the barn's doorway
a bull emerges quietly
through a cloud of gnats

Late night poker game
Caracas, Venezuela
under a bare bulb

Rabbit tobacco
rolled up in brown paper bag
smoked by all my kin

Brittle is happy
but Tough As Nails is grouchy
Careful's with Brittle

Using that pinched voice
to mock people complaining
means they might should have

Mouse pawprints in soot
across the cold fireplace hearth
Vacant shack, winter

The orchid hunter
brings his disinterested son
who's texting his friends

Clattering teeth toy
careens across the table
hell bent for the edge

Pragmatic wizard
Not practicing alchemy
Prospecting instead

Train comes off the rails
Boxcars gouge into the ground
Throw up dirt and rocks

Monster in the drain
cloaked in matted hair and gunk
Eats your spent toothpaste

Our flags on the Moon
have no breeze to flutter in
plus, they've faded white

Package tied with string
Near the fence at the White House
Bomb robot creeps up

His jokes are clumsy
difficult to react to
with a clear-cut laugh

Siren test postponed
due to inclement weather
Could be heard as real

Squirrel's road crossing plan:
First run, then stop, flick your tail,
panic, run crazy

Archaeologist
digs up a Lincoln penny
Thinks "Who was Lincoln?"

Curse of The Simpsons
53 voices have died
after guest starring

Electricity
Just lightning, eels, and static,
until "discovered"

Under my front seat
Pink Bad Company 8-track
and some old SweeTarts

A 5-year-old boy
whacks at shrubs in the front yard
with a broom handle

Had some vindaloo
Served leftovers to my dog
Dog went "Aack aack aack"

Man with a stern face
like Easter Island sculptures
Runs the ice cream shop

I know karate
I can "Man from U.N.C.L.E." you
if you misbehave

"Goat Man" of Georgia
moved his herd down country roads
Rumored to be rich

Ant to ant warning
"If you cross that countertop,
thumbs will mash you flat"

I'm so impatient
I glare at the microwave
and go "Hurry up !!"

Birds hate early Spring
The feeders go empty but
there's nothing to eat

They covered your face
before you were really dead
Throw back the sheet, glare

The tired butterfly
rests on a blanket of snow
Didn't make it south

The sprinkler system
above the Mona Lisa
is poised and ready

You'll pick Mighty Mouse
if you've come to save the day
but have no theme song

Faded billboard clouds
wish they were dark like storm clouds
that roar into town

Old woman sweeping
Her broom worn down to a nub
makes ruts in the dust

At Drivers Ed school
Ralph finds the simulator
has bumper car mode

The natty possum
feels downy and attractive
after a Spring rain

The moon comes in close
So close it brushes treetops
and tides go haywire

Act Eleven: Jaded Punk

Chess club in Heaven
Gandhi/Benjamin Franklin
Jim Morrison/Saul

Jaded punk rock girl
says things like "I hate that band"
then goes shoplifting

It's a real wet rain
The kind that pools in your shoes
and makes pine trees fall

Tea was discovered
Then other leaves were brewed up
without much success

This made the bear's day
A 5-lb. bag of sugar
left on a tailgate

Hovering boulder
casts a shadow on the ground
just inches below

Practice basketball
Dribble out the window of
a slow-moving car

Lay down, close your eyes
Count backwards from a thousand
by threes, get sleepy

Sailors who lost limbs
Assigned duties like mess cook
on ships of the line

On my next pizza
A drizzle of maple syrup,
salt, and lemon juice

Star Trek films in Taos
It's too expensive to film
on other planets

1561
Space battle in the morning
over Nuremberg

Oak leaf impression
Sunk shallow in the concrete
There for good, leaf's gone

Walk by a nice car
Swoop in close to the window
Make shade with your hand

Indian pickles
My description's off-putting
"Tastes like turpentine"

He yells "Incoming!!"
She turns around just in time
to see the baseball

Proof it might storm soon
Birds fly low, wind's unruly,
shadows disappear

Specter flies at night
can't see the clothes line at all
Gets sliced right in half

Campus mockingbird
Class lets out, protects its nest,
darts at everyone

Man turns over rocks
looking for that spare house key
in the pouring rain

Crook looks through garbage
to steal credit card numbers
Doesn't trust the Web

Don't breathe in the dust
when you shred poison ivy
in the wood chipper

Vegetarian
crocodiles make much softer
boots, handbags, and belts

Going back in time
and killing a bug or bugs
is probably OK

Seldom gets enjoyed
Pictures of space on spaceships
hung in crew quarters

"Spend most of their time
running from special effects,"
said the bad reviews

Swing swings by itself
and there's been no one around
for several hours

Our white azaleas
look great for a few days, then...
like dirty diapers

On the ocean floor
lays silent the ride cymbal
from the Titanic

This guy's saxophone
has a nagging style and tone
like a clown car's horn

Water pistol jammed
after I filled it up with
gritty pond water

Found as a fossil
A Commodore 64
Unearthed, Tulsa Dig

Change hiking trail plaques
to show not deer and rabbits
but werewolves and trolls

Guy sets his tea down
Blows pollen with his blower
Tea gets yellow film

Kid wants to draw ghosts
Decides to use stick figures
drawn with dotted lines

Maple syrup and salt
Top notch in homemade oatmeal
Not the chef's mistake

You point your finger
Cats look at your fingertip
Not at where you point

My car's a bucket
Oil leaks, windows won't roll down,
volume's stuck on loud

Keep your Beatles wig
in the original bag
Don't wear it around

For our first breakfast
I wanted all our cracked eggs
to be double yoked

Micro fiber shirt
Very soft but doesn't breathe
Get hot, you stay hot

World's biggest "city"
An ant's nest that stretches from
Portugal through Spain

I'll always refuse
nettles, pine straw, maggot cheese,
liver, and creamer

Ancient sculpture found
Giant head of a storm god
Looks like Wayne Rooney

The sun's in my eyes
If I close them I see red
and all my floaters

Don't buy those shoes now
I hear they're going on sale
in about a week

Gravity's Rainbow
Finished it at a deli
sitting in a booth

We call things "butter"
like easy jigsaw puzzles
and, of course, butter

Tree fell on my car
and the haiku in my head
evaporated

I wear my hair net
at the Twinkies factory
because I have to

Sure: S U R E
or sure: S H U R E
Second one seems right

Chiropractic school
If you show up with a limp
everyone's on you

Ronald McDonald
plays maracas in my band
Suit, tie, slicked back hair

They have a salt lick
on the dining room table
Scrape some off with spoons

Write words in the dust
Don't clean it or anything
Just write words in it

Stayed at the table
Mom made me finish my squash
Missed Roller Derby

Send a message up
The mothership floats in space
Thrusters off, waiting

Nothing personal
(Well, uh, actually it is)
Your soup tastes like paint

Don Quixote's lance
bobbles over Sancho's head
as they ride along

3 in the morning
Teen sneaks around trying doors
in his neighborhood

She makes handmade soaps
and on a good night she dreams
about handmade soaps

Offer a house plant
Not a human sacrifice
Might appease, might not

"The Longest Journey"
"Starman" and "A Band Called Death"
All make me teary

School's atomic drill
Third grade, crouched under my desk
Saw a roach crawl by

Using a thimble
the resourceful hummingbird
fashions a stout nest

Front row seats at Cream
with my crewcut, Sunday suit
and penny loafers

Strip mining dump truck
Vandalized and up on blocks
Radio's gone too

When one wire comes loose
the coffee maker timer
tries to start a fire

Stone crushing machine
spreads them out, gives our driveway
a nice get home sound

Grey ball from my mouse
with nice hefty weight to it
is great for throwing

Spanish explorers
sliced up by the palmettos
wilt in stifling heat

Aim with a mirror
Try to hit the Coke can "o"
Annie Oakley style

Local drug dealer,
when the Foghat album ends,
hears police dogs bark

I

Dissident kitchen
Borscht, radishes, shades pulled down
Plotting in whispers

II

KGB agent
hides in the stairwell listening
to their spoons clinking

Park deer graze at dusk
We walk right up and pet them
on their hard brown heads

Stinkin' unicorn's
knockin' apples off my tree
with its stinkin' horn

Folding metal chairs
in a field for a wedding
getting super-hot

My friend hates the beach
When she has to go she pouts
Sits facing the land

Good slicing advice
Halve grape tomatoes long ways
Less squishing, trust me

Act Twelve: Clucking Kids

Kids cluck like chickens
when Hypnosis Club lets out
and they all get home

Bird perched on a branch
Loses its balance briefly
Flaps wings, regains grip

International
"Don't Freeze" sign is a red slash
across a penguin

Jetsons walk Astro
on their treacherous treadmill
30 stories up

Kimchi's terrible
on hot dogs, surprisingly
since sauerkraut's great

Bolivian punks
mope past the street market stalls
in Black Flag t-shirts

Losing altitude
the basket on the balloon
bounces off our roof

Browsing the book store
Ice cream you forgot about's
melting in the trunk

Bat flies through a swarm
of mosquitoes, mouth open
like a whale eats krill

The color-blind girl's
amazing coloring book
Wows the neighbor kids

Clumsy gardener
often times will drag the hose
over tender plants

First the baby bird
dodges getting run over
then hides by the curb

George Armstrong Custer
sleeps with his pistol strapped on
because he sleepwalks

Porcelain Santas
Languish, top shelf, hall closet
Until they're needed

Vibrations move vase
to the edge of the table
inch by patient inch

To keep it secret
Chipmunk runs past it's burrow
and hides in the shrubs

Shunned at the buffet
Lime Jell-O with carrot bits
suspended in it

All termites concur
Pine's the enticing flavor
and plywood's pablum

Intricate tunnels
carved by termites eating through
a box of paper

Chain smoking Camels
the obsessive man tunes in
to the police band

Brushed chrome VCR
A 70's prototype
Big as a suitcase

Honey never spoils
Discovered in King Tut's tomb
Gross, but edible

Guy drives down the road
Bare arm hangs out the window
Passenger's does too

What you had for lunch
shows up in your fingerprints
as trace elements

Enterprising wren
uses a nail as a spear
to ward off a hawk

Stranded icebreaker
Hundreds of testy penguins
approach raising Cain

Funeral's over
Black clad relatives bring ham
back to the cold house

Pear tree knocked over
by strong winds during a storm
blossoms one last time

The choir director
plays Schoenberg piano works
when no one's around

Pizza cooks feed birds
with broken up, fresh-baked crusts
during the blizzard

CSI, the Moon
Footprints stay sharp in the dust
but droplets float off

Thrift store puzzle shelf
Many loose pieces scattered
on the floor below

For the reunion
Dad dons the white boots he wore
with Mott the Hoople

Lightning rods installed
on house, barn, church, boat, or car
Call for estimate

One last torpedo
through sailors in the water
finishes the ship

Number 56
Ants Climbing Tree, I'll try that
Is it very hot?

Car, no insurance,
brake light busted, blinker on,
seatbelt off, and drunk

Crows are like people
after the apocalypse
Just take, take, take, take

Teenage lightning bug
stays out all night still flashing
when the sun comes up

Flea market landscape
Pink moon reflects in the lake
$13.95

Bears spook some campers
then sit around their campfire
Not sure what to do

Under the pine trees
brittle brambles wait, patient
for the drought to end

The train robber's horse
matches the baggage car's speed
Doesn't see the bridge

Pool party's over
She's passed out on the chaise lounge
Sun sets, rain moves in

Play a soft gong note
Hit it right in the center
Get a boomy tone

Bird feeder has holes
Empty plastic BB pack
found outside the fence

For your punishment
you'll carry a cinder block
around for a year

2025
Vending machines have NewTwix
Tiny and 12 bucks

Pot boils over - Hiss!
Cook runs in from the den - Crash!
Tripped on the rug — Ow!

Wise Salad Master
scrutinizes every piece
Frets about textures

2 bicyclists
stopped, posing identical,
chugging Gatorade

Sat up late, slept late
Woke with sleepy in my eyes
Pillow creases too

The crook in the tree
traps a little dirt, and weeds
try for a foothold

Dashed into the road
to snatch up the dire turtle
while traffic bore down

First one down the path
clears the spider webs and strands
with his face and neck

Act Thirteen: Pink Suits

Bird shows off to friends
Whizzes so low to the ground
wing tips kick up leaves

Kid gets just one track
with his model Panther tank
Writes the company

While mowing the yard
hummed Baby Elephant Walk
over and over

Puts on his pink suit
black shirt, red tie, expects stares
at church and Church's

"I'm low on arrows"
Cupid complains to Venus
"and I want some pants"

Tired of grease duty
Apprentice barbecuer
dreams of mixing sauce

Big brash horn section
powers the high school soul band
tearing up the prom

She loves her yoga
Mats, leotards, beach retreats
She may quit her job

Snow on my lawn chairs
piled high looking like some clouds
sitting there resting

Lawman has gun drawn
The lynch mob draws near the jail
where Outlaw Drew's held

Airplanes of Popeye
Wing fabric can be pulled off
and they still fly fine

Graceful water bug
relies on surface tension
to stand on the lake

Boyd's Apple Outlet
Closed, boarded up, parking lot
overgrown with weeds

Kid looks up to think
Leaves fountain pen on crossword
Looks down, big blue stain

I

My car's horn got stuck
so now it blows constantly
All my trips are bad

II

I recited this
to my wife when I got home
She thought MY horn broke

Suspicious shopper
Clerk dials 9, 1, leaves hand poised
over the last 1

My pet squirrel Nosey
loved almonds but hated Mom
because she vacuumed

Office building built
on ancient burial grounds
Much calling in sick

Persnicketiness
It's NOT "a gift... and a curse"
It's a honkin' GIFT!!

Parking lot, K-Mart
White faced Goth kids wear black capes
in the July heat

DANGER OPEN WELL
Faded sign tacked to a tree
stopped us in our tracks

Japanese punk girl
does the tea ceremony
with surprising ease

Badger craves thistle
Sips rank creek water like wine
Likes the finer things

World record sky dive
He jumped from the edge of space
Fell so long got bored

Smart and Ninety-Nine
scuba diving, encounter
Kaos mini-subs

Her mood turns gloomy
at every single sunset
She dreads the night so

Street light PD10
Wonder what PD stands for ?
Maybe it's Preet Dight

Locals brought picnics
to the Battle of Bull Run
and watched from high ground

I

Smokejumper's thermos
Dented, singed, paint flecked off
Worked many a fire

II

Girlfriend of Smoky
A Hello Kitty thermos
Pink, lives on a shelf

My wife's pointing out
our unmowed yard's like that show
Life After People

The shy groundhog finds
a dense briar patch to hide in
while the Brownies pass

Wishywashyville
Population 25
Maybe 24

Steamy mist hovers
over wet summer asphalt
Tang of oil and dirt

Old car parked in front
of a Kansas City bank
it's engine running

Sir Pothole, the knight
with his orange road cone helmet
and his Stop sign shield

Tropical airstrip
Cessna hit with 12 arrows
Decides not to land

Beach glass collection
brown; Bud, green; Mountain Dew, blue;
Milk of Magnesia

Shut-in dies in bed
A hint of rain approaching
Breeze moves the curtains

Hugely inventive
Kid plays spy in the front yard
Completely alone

Ants find long blonde hairs
They weave them into a mat
to drag more food home

For a while nothing
Then suddenly there's something
Then nothing again

Sky Bucket 13
"No," says the Mom at 6 Flags
with 3 rowdy kids

Frugal man's house shoes
held together with duct tape
good for one more fall

Cat naps in a swing
most all day in a backyard
no one goes out in

The landing party
will soon materialize
at the beheading

Spider has a leaf
snared by a few strands of web
Flies it like a kite

The poor white crayon
is very much underused
by most colorers

A pillow that purrs
when you rest your head on it
Huge retail success

Ace story teller
can summon claps of thunder
to hold attention

Scourge of all farm kids
Pick blackberries, get redbugs
Toothpicks pry them off

Slave graves, rock headstones
Dry brown leaves surround each mound
right inside the woods

I scrapped the haiku
about conniving dolphins.
I was forcing it.

Etiquette problem
Pointing with your fried chicken
especially the leg

Vietnamese boys
plot their fighting beetle match
while they're having pho

Tree branch reaches down
gently touches a tombstone
This takes 20 years

I crack my window
instead of trying to swat
the bug in my car

Rats, I have no cash
Could you spot me two dollars
for an espresso?

She messed up the sink
dyeing her hair bright chartreuse
before her big date

A screen door opens
with that wooden squeeek, then SLAMS
with that loose rattle

Plane changes its mind
Leaves a U-shaped vapor trail
and goes somewhere else

Thick smoke fills the house
but the alarm doesn't sound
Old 9 volt tries though

The sundowner yells
obscenities and insults
Starts about 7

Ants walk on the film
that's developed on water
that's been still for weeks

Like Medusa's head
I carry the dug up stump
held high to the trash

Most 60's fight scenes
get bongo accompaniment
unless they're Westerns

She paints in her car
A gentle landscape she sees
while rain patters down

Photo shoot canceled
Scaffolding at the castle
would ruin the postcard

Act Fourteen: Eden's Tall Grass

I ordered sun dae
but our Korean waitress
said "Try something else"

Snakes in the tall grass
have ruined our sunny field romp
Now we're just running

A leaf hides the star
so just move your head slightly
It'll reappear

The trapeze artist
wrings his hands on the platform
lacking confidence

Whiff of gunpowder
hangs in the Minute Market
after the shootout

I've got cold church hands
If I hold hands with my wife
in the pew, she'll flinch

Use a microscope
to view heartbeats in the ink
Forgers write slowly

Dear (insert name here)
I'm a Nigerian prince
with money troubles

Beware of straight pins
wedged in the carpet point up
in the dressing room

The robot sneezes
Sounds like a stapler stapling
Little oil comes out

Dad dug up my men
buried in their shallow graves
Army men, that is

NASA found comets
stink, like rotten eggs and poop
Asteroids like pee

Shorthand crackerjack
"You talk as fast as you want,
I've got every word"

My stern grandfather
still in his scratchy wool coat
sits near the wood stove

Guy smells like Playdough
Might be an odd new cologne
or he's been baking

Point leaf blower up
to make loose leaves fall in Fall
Less raking later

It's 15 below
and the koi pond has frozen
Snow blows across it

Debbie pops popcorn
while a tornado bears down
on her modest home

Family panic-runs
through the park in egg sized hail
Coats over their heads

Amazing brass band
plays while riding bicycles
No wrong notes or spills

Little leak and drip
fills the submarine captain's
shoes while he's sleeping

Puff of acid smoke
spurts from my steering column
while I'm still in park

Boy notices girl
Both walk like Neanderthals
Meant for each other

Drops of mercury
pushed around by lunch room kids
with their plastic forks

At the Guggenheim
a crowd admires a ladder
propped against the wall

Squid leaves a black swirl
as it squirts away from fish
who snap at the ink

Aunt Viv won the prize
Free cremation at Pine Hill
Tupperware urn too

With a strong light source
he checks for double yoked eggs
they can charge more for

Got a .22
for Christmas. Yeaaa!! Can't shoot it
in the backyard though.

President Carter
leaning back disappointed
in his leather chair

Bum's got a banjo
and a pistol just in case
no one likes banjo

Chord sounds like a smile

Play it softly glancing up
at your listener

"The Song of Blow Up"
sung by demolition crews
all across the South

Spirit of Lou Reed
with arms outstretched ascending
into his heaven

Toy six shooter drawn
Broomstick horse kicking up dust
He's rootin'-tootin'

Trudging through the snow
Black dog in a red sweater
approaching the church

Tintin reads Lovecraft
and is off to Providence
to scoop the Old Ones

Crow plays in the snow
Rolls downhill with wings tucked in
over and over

Corn maze 3 AM
Couple makes 911 call
Lost, left there, first date

John Lennon records
a clever message on his
answering machine

"Squeaky wheel gets oil"
Sure, but soon you shop for wheels
that don't squeak at all

Stan, stressed out freshman
joins the Hammock Club at school
Becomes president

Machete glinting
in the sun as the guide hacks
a path through the vines

Bulldog eats a bee
trudges over to its bowl
and laps up water

Tornado logo
has a mischievous smile
and angry eyebrows

My custom ring tone
Tolling bell of a buoy
in the friendless fog

Rugged dandelion
pushes up green and yellow
through December snow

Bigfoot throws huge rocks
angrily into the lake
splashing my canoe

Act Fifteen: Gypsy Caravan

Gypsy caravan
camped on the hospital green
Queen's in with gall stones

Before smoke alarms
my parents put firecrackers
above every door

The Christmas Dragon
hovers flamelessly above
kids on their new bikes

Um-um-um-varoom!!
A car's clock will stop briefly
as the engine's cranked

Guy's got Devo hair
plus wears a red leisure suit
at most occasions

Blurs in the Fall sky
over our house in Macon
Hummingbirds streak south

"Believe it or not,
I sleep the sleep of the just"
said the Minotaur

Gold sparkle drum set
in front of a green curtain
on a pink carpet

Abandoned silo
My Geiger counter crackles
and my scalp tingles

What makes me cringe most
is cutting into staples
not nails on chalkboards

"We're part of the flock"
Hawk drafts behind our Honda
as we're driving home

First a long skid mark
then a charcoal black burn spot
near the overpass

An alien race
covered in ultra clean hair
call themselves The Prell

Stiff neck? Turn torso
to look to the left or right
like Frankenstein would

Dropped potato chip
crumbs in my dress shirt pocket
Greasy stain sets in

Dinosaurs trumpet
loud and sustained like hot rods
revving down the road

My shadow appears
in the photograph I took
of the Spanish Steps

Spooky rendition,
whistled, of "I Saw Mommy
Kissing Santa Claus"

The Archangel perched
on a moss-covered boulder
watching a coiled snake

She's so determined
yet her opinions are vague
and ignorable

Love Kay's Kiss parties
Her refurbished smoke machine
fills the house knee deep

Bob stole laughing gas
from the dentist down the street
That was some weekend

Lowlife calls his wife
Says "I'm in Paulding County"
She knows he's in jail

Frosty morning fog
billows across the farm yard
with notes of burnt wood

Girl feeds crows for years
In return they bring her gifts
Paper clips, twine, twigs...

My Finnigans Wake
Support Group meets on Tuesdays
One page at a time

A circle of men
stand in a steady downpour
around the fresh corpse

The choir sings "Onward
Christian so oh oh ger uhrs
marching as to war"

9 looked like a 4
so, the layaway's paid off
months ahead of time

Clown stands in the trees
Looks keenly across the park
for picnics to join

I
Darwin searched for bugs
with snouts long enough to reach
star orchid nectar

II
40 years later
the hawk moth is discovered
Sports that very snout

When my parrot bites
it feels like you've been pinched hard
by needle nose pliers

I

WOMEN USED FLOUR SACKS
TO MAKE THEIR DAUGHTERS' DRESSES
1935

II

SO, FLOUR COMPANIES
BEGAN PRODUCING THE SACKS
IN COLORS AND PRINTS

JUMBO PAPER CLIPS
DO RESEMBLE TROMBONE SLIDES
AND PUSH PINS THE MUTES

50 caliber
shell casings litter the road
Binh Ba '69

Hard core Sun Ra fan
buys his spoken word album
where he explains space

View Earth from a world
millions of light years away
See triceratops

Sow seeds, mend the fence,
close the gate, and then hum Bach's
Sheep May Safely Graze

Worst yard sale ever
Just empty mayonnaise jars
and soy sauce bottles

Angry raccoon pinned
under the tipped over top
of our bird bath

Young rehab patients
flock around the older guy
who was at Woodstock

Girl from LA froze
They're blasting at the quarry
and the ground rumbled

A rabbit couple
sitting on the knoll at night
watch the moon through clouds

In a shrill manner
performed "Morning has Broken"
on the recorder

SPACE SHUTTLE SNAGS KITE
Florida Today headline
2/9/98

Grandpa remembers
when I-285
was just one level

Bride sits on the hood
posing in her wedding dress
She loves that Mustang

Now available
Hot sauce with hornet venom
called Stings from the Hole

Kurt Cobain's Visa
sold at auction for thousands
It's signed "check id"

I've bent my Slinky
Now it's a tangle of wire
and good for nothing

When I see a snake
I wonder how much it weighs
so, I pick it up

American flag
done up in light browns and greys
flies over the land fill

Act Fifteen: Rainy Day Sunrise

Sunrise doesn't care
if you look down at your feet
or look up in awe

Rainy day Sunday
and we're on the expressway
with wipers that smear

Mouse moves stealthy slow
Tries not to sway the tall grass
in case a hawk's near

My spry haiku mouse
will do whatever I say
like "Don't sway that grass"

Andy Carroll falls
off a barstool in London
at 7am

Puppy growls at me
when I try to take the stick
of butter from him

Ice cream truck from Hell
backfiring and burning oil
serves cayenne dipped cones

Clown has room for rent
He'll keep you up all night though
blowing taxi horns

VW van
with surf boards strapped to the roof
Jan & Dean blaring

I

Tornado rips through
the ping pong ball factory
Thousands fill the sky

II

Hours later bounce down
into streets of nearby towns
trilling the children

How can we prove that
your orange might be my purple
or my green your blue

Hammers and feathers...
They do fall at the same speed
on the airless Moon

Sir Isaac Newton
draws equations in the sand
with his walking stick

Above our doorbell
I wrote PUSH THE BUTTON...
AND SEE THE GORILLA

I'm first to arrive
and notice 3 coyotes
prowl the parking lot

With baby in tow
Heavy Metal Mom and Dad
Browse Ozzie albums

Spinning and grinning
The knife thrower's assistant's
mind's strangely at ease

I'm not outdoorsy
I use the outside mainly
to get to my car

Hawk hits the window
Leaves a bird shaped smudge, complete
with a surprised look

My least favorite friend
lights up when he gets the chance
to hassle someone

Red paint covered Earth
That Sherwin Williams logo
worried me, age 4

Euell Gibbons' salad
features kudzu and thistle
with thousand island

Twister mat flies off
sucked out of a mobile home
by a tornado

I feed the chipmunks
"Those almonds smell like people"
is their main complaint

The arrogant poet
doesn't bother counting syllables
for his haiku poems

Sea otters hold hands
to keep from floating apart
while they nap at sea

We grow prize catnip
often finding local cats
asleep between rows

Zombies roam the town
as comet dust showers down
Sadly, one's a clown

Made popcorn at work
with extra salt and butter
My keyboard's greasy

Got jacks for Christmas
"What in the world do I do
with them and that ball"

I have a headache
but I'm trying to enjoy
my weekend in Spite

My hovering hand
above my keyboard searching
for the question mark

A murder mystery
in 17 syllables
bang hide found trial jail

House foreclosed upon
Homemade jellies left dusty
on the window sill

Play chess with all pawns
Whole new strategies evolve
with much attrition

Guy bought a Les Paul
Replaced the gold strap buttons
with swing set eye bolts

Star Fleet's requirements
for crew immunizations
is EXTREMELY long

Paint by numbers cloud
1 is blue and 2 is white
Doesn't take too long

The Jack Benny look
Arms crossed, fingertips touch cheek,
black suit, thin black tie

I play bass trumpet
Not much call for bass trumpet
I practice, and wait

Silently the ship
settles on the ocean floor
in a swirl of sand

Duck hunters take aim
at a hovering spaceship
out over the lake

Don Rickles scowling
in his third-grade class picture
foretells his success

Lost Andy Griffith
Opie runs away from home
and joins the circus

To sit up all night
have 2 Styrofoam cups of
Mountain Dew at 10

"The Bull-Headed Daughter"

I

Mom asks the speech coach
"My child calls her doll Husan."
"Can she say Susan ?"

II

The speech coach replies
"Sure, but that's really its name
and she won't change it"

I

Breakneck air battles
at the hummingbird feeder
No one sips for long

II

They don't realize
we've a pound bag of sugar
so, they battle on

Sun gets right to work
on crushed ice slug from my cup
in the parking lot

Little short haired mutt
wound up tight runs through the house
with dog tags jangling

Day after vodka
I apologize for Hyde
but Jekyll bought it

Two butterflies land
and square off to fight a duel
armed with pine needles

Class paints Coke bottles
Teacher adds sprinkler nozzles
Gifts for Moms who iron

My nemesis died
Got a souvenir hand fan
from the funeral

Huge flock of seagulls
hovering in front of us
as we sling Cheetos

My cadaver dog
whimpers and paces about
when I thaw a steak

I make the best dip
for darts, from orange and black frogs
I find in the trees

Act Sixteen: Hard Garbage Sprays

Walk briskly through leaves
being blown sideways by wind
preceding a storm

Dumpster slammed down, wham
Garbage truck backs off, beep beep
as the sun comes up

My first liver spot
right on the tip of my nose
and shaped like a heart

Hard sprays of water
as depth charges gouge the hull
and open up seams

I

Ants dig out garnets
Discard them around their hill
deeming them worthless

II

Until they warm up
Then they're brought back in that night
to keep their eggs warm

I

Christmas '61
New electric football set
with green metal field

II

Both sets of players
head straight for the sidelines though
when I turn it on

Little do they know
as brain cells fire one last time
that you've been poisoned

Rogue Amazon drone
I get home and my package
is up on the roof

At the kid's table
Timmie hates his baked chicken
Yells "I found a vein !!"

She wants a crater
on the Moon named after me
Small one would be fine

Monkey loves fish sticks
Uses my toaster oven
and watches them cook

Most leaves need raking
but curly willow leaves fall
and disintegrate

My Scout friends dared me
"Have a sip of stump water"
Tastes like iced coffee

Old witch churns butter
Turns out flaky, pale, and sour
which is what she likes

Crawl out of the surf
after a jellyfish sting
Shaky and alone

The bull shark just ate
so, it swam past my cousin
on his air mattress

The bucket brigade
slips and slides on muddy ground
because they slosh so

Switched on the rain room
Went in with our prototype
paper umbrella

Ruler company
finds out their inch is too short
and brace for lawsuits

James Brown just fired me
from his band... and they've left me
at the bus station

I

Farm kids sneak some smokes
in the corn field while Pa plows
the next plot over

II

Youngest shouts "A bear!!"
They drop everything and bolt
Field burns that evening

For better pho broth
add dissolved Good 'n' Plentys
2 whites and 1 pink

Unkept pool at dusk
Loudest frog claims the top step
on the chrome ladder

Call of the barred owl
sounds to me like a hound dog
doing vaudeville tunes

My shrink-wrap machine
saves huge amounts of money
Regifting's a breeze

The first Sphinx paint job
was wildly psychedelic
like a Peter Max

Johnny plays blues harp
along with my Beethoven
Symphony records

I fell like a clown
Hard on my behind, feet up,
with akimbo arms

Order sea urchin
and taste essence of ocean
much like a tide pool

Cranked up my old van
Drove stop start about 2 blocks
Failed my emissions

The Moon has a moon
the size of an M&M
not the peanut kind

With murder in mind
She's in the jungle looking
for tiger whiskers

Teenage boy's haiku
Coffins float in flood water
Gives it to his girl

Cows bothered by flies
They swarm thick around her nose
and her tail won't reach

The feral children
leave piles of cracked open shells
in my peanut field

Drive-in, doobie smoke,
horror flick, Police dog bark,
sudden flashlight glare

What robots can't do
yet is sort and fold laundry
They just wad it up

Paul Bunyan's breath froze
Dropped to the ground like ice cubes
he kicked like gravel

I'm on a planet
covered pole to pole with tacks
all pointing outwards

"I litter boulders"
said the retreating glacier
"anywhere I please."

Little baby skunk,
cutest of all the babies
at the petting zoo

Numskull drives to work
eating a TV dinner
Steering with his knees

To pick up paper
with a sharp pair of scissors
takes many attempts

The aging hipster
wears a slouchy black beret
on his shiny head

At Goth Jamboree
my blackened lamb hearts won gold
and my punch silver

Old man loves free jazz
Blasts it at his nursing home
to others' dismay

Leaf hangs from a web
like masking tape on glass doors
you shouldn't walk through

Our deaf child Ruth signs
and our nodding family dog
seems to understand

Revenge is a dish
best to add Limburger to
so, it's real stinky

Scarecrow has 10 eyes
which is unnerving to us
Crows too, probably

Ghost chilis are hot
but these new Chernobyl reds
will glow in the dark

Smoking while shaving
One cough, one nick, blames the first
Camel of the day

Rush t-shirt, spare tire,
plaid boxers, pale legs, black socks,
brown sandals, Big Gulp

The rain hammers down
The hippos approach the boat
Our guide grabs his gun

Two eyes reflect back
She drops her flashlight and squirms
from under the house

Kid can't swallow pills
Mom hides one in a brownie
yum yum yum crunch aaack

Act Seventeen: Into the Blizzard

"Throw-away-able"
What she calls my lame haiku
about Dracula

Four girls in parkas
drive a white convertible
into the blizzard

She shows up in court
with magic marker makeup
and zipped up hoodie

Old timey sling shot
and carefully aimed paint balls
defeats the blue team

Leaves outside reflect
off the tv's picture tube
in our empty den

Walking Dead billboard
above a funeral home
Detroit, Michigan

Andre the Giant
sits on a smaller wrestler
and winks at the crowd

Scarecrow gets his brain
but returning to Kansas
just hangs out in fields

I
Taste of an apple
Little white little yellow
little red and green

II
Wife says "Needs more punch...
and what about the texture
and snap of the peel."

III
Excel feels regret
about the spreadsheet error
in 2020

IV
Again, Wife says "No,
it doesn't quite get across
the A.I. concept."

The first Saint from Mars
brought health care to the natives
in the red clay caves

My nephew dabbles
on the dark internet sites
with the curtains pulled

The bedroom mirror
distracts the demon inching
toward our son's crib

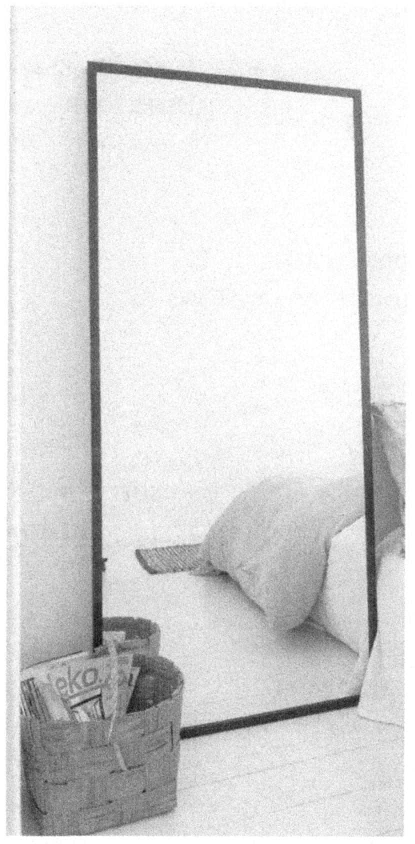

Piano teacher
has old New Yorkers for kids
to read while they wait

Buddha meanders
through the warm but mundane world
with no need for sleep

Cherry blossoms fall
I'M AN OLD COWHAAAND!!, Oh crap!!
That's stuck in my head

Crows keep track of time
using the sundial's shadow
but not it's numbers

Atmosphere's worn out
and won't conduct vibrations
at all anymore

Barry Manilow
sued by a concert goer
claiming hearing loss

Offer safety tips
Get a 10-mile argument
from the smug driver

I

Chimps slide down the slide
on the abandoned playground
in Tanzania

II

Then throw up their hands,
squeal with delight, climb back up
and slide down again

I

"Don't walk to the stream.
The path's infested with snakes,
water moccasins."

II

Both our eyes go wide
We'd just trudged down there looking
up at Spanish moss

While Mammoths still roamed
pyramids were being built
down south in Egypt

Tiring cliff climber
hooked onto the rusty pin
tapped in years ago

Walk leaning forward
Keep both arms straight down, fists clenched,
frown, and don't blink much

When I say I'm bored
my daydreaming has shut down
and that's serious

Gravy sleeper cell
activated by the phrase
"Gravy Boat Alpha"

The movie Trainwreck
has ruined Google Image Search
you know, for train wrecks

Toddler stops and grabs
a fuzzy caterpillar
Screams that day long scream

Kenyan student's goat
slaughtered in the dorm stairwell
Concrete steps hosed off

He adjusts blinds well
So well in fact neighbors ask
"Will you adjust our's?"

Rainy night in Stoke
Arsenal's trailing 1 - nil
Crowd's on Wenger's back

Ground unicorn horn
makes race horses nearly fly
and wink like cute girls

Deer jump every night
Wear holes in our trampoline
with their pointy hooves

Man in a hurry
walks spry with a full coffee
Spills a bit each step

Male butterflies feed
on drops of blood in the woods
after a bear fight

I
Hospital barber:
"Does the patient in room 10
have any cowlicks?"

II
HIPAA rules: "DON'T TELL !!"
so that's just one bad haircut
waiting to happen

Thai rice terrace kids
play hide and seek like Kirk plays
3D chess with Spock

Musicologists
in 2525
revive that chestnut

Obscure gipsy curse
"From now on your fingertips
will smell like cat pee"

Robinson Crusoe
first thinks it's a shooting star
Then it circles back

It's the growing point
where the stem meets the radish
you should always eat

Berserker's sword blades
are sharp dull sharp dull sharp dull
for a jagged slice

Swindler's flame red hair
matched perfectly his jump suit
as he picked up trash

Our band's half time show
was ruined by the away crowd
who all blew whistles

Wore my friend's glasses
Made me look like John Lennon
Got the worst headache

"Why's that mouse painting
framed and hung down near the floor?"
"We used to have cats."

I play Messerschmitt
armed with my water pistol
shooting down fire flies

D-Day veteran
bothered by even postcards
that show sandy beach

How to best leave town
Lean back hard on the head rest
Wave a parade wave

No flu shot this year
I'll just wash my hands a lot
and breathe less deeply

Sweet Potato Jones
runs a sweet potato farm
Yes, that's her real name

Cell phone blasts out "Help!"
a clever Beatles ring tone
If you're in quicksand

Loose fitting white robe
hinders jumping for his hood
caught up in a tree

For your cat's birthday
Wrap a box of bugs with string
Place it on the floor

Act Eighteen: More Eden's Tall Grass

A cloud in our house
confirms that air everywhere
is part of the sky

Mountaineering class
climbs the Bellamy Building
at Florida State

Cold day, no one home
The old ghost summons up strength
and turns on the stove

The wife sliced lemons
for the beekeeper's breakfast
and served them on toast

Constantly damp socks
turned feet waxy and ashen
while deployed in Nam

The lp's last groove
is circular with the sound
of a ringing phone

If you call yourself
a stalwart of the hip scene
You're not a stalwart

It's time to remove
Linda Blair's milky contacts
so she can have lunch

Impatient faxer
groans his document isn't
in Korea yet

Cobbler get clobbered
when he refuses to mend
some Converse All-Stars

The Tic-Tock Man's nose
is the button you pull out
to set the alarm

Neither snow nor rain
nor sleet nor gloom of night, well...
OK maybe snow

MULTI-ARMED MONSTER
AT YOUR BEDSIDE WHILE YOU SLEEP
JUST WANTS TO HOLD HANDS

? SHOULDN'T QUESTION MARKS
BE IN FRONT OF THE SENTENCE.
YOU'D KNOW WHAT'S COMING

? WANT THE LIGHT TO CHANGE
JUST START REORGANIZING
YOUR GLOVE COMPARTMENT

WHERE DRAGONS TOUCH DOWN
NOTHING WILL GROW FOR SIX YEARS
OR SOMETIMES SEVEN

My desk's so dusty
Post-It notes won't even stick
Scotch tape won't either

Happy bees hover
around the honey man's booth
and bother no one

Everyone's late to work
Little do they know the Earth
spins slower today

I swipe a saucer
from my sister's new tea set
to dig for earthworms

Student film makers
approach the shunned haunted house
Ghosts say "Finally"

Old rocking horse toy
both eyes painted solid white
Looks like it's from Hell

Chengdu Pandamen
beat Hong Kong Combat Orcas
14 to 7

Pedaling like mad
chased down the trail by a bear
and getting winded

With my six shooter
rubber band gun I settle
past injustices

The fungus creature
at last breaks free from damp ground
and plods toward town

While Claude Monet paints
worms work their way through rich soil
below his easel

Best baked potatoes
are served topped with plain yogurt
and red caviar

Half inflated raft
floats just below the surface
found by the Coast Guard

Knowing the print's forged
the auctioneer's shaky voice
sparks little interest

Tipoverables
That's what I call top heavy
plants in the back seat

On playing Webern
"I've seen these notes before, just
not in this order"

Huge knockdowndragout
coming from our neighbor's house
on Christmas morning

Our office pool swells
Distant webcam eagle squats
on her unhatched eggs

Largest spray I've seen
was when the tracks were submerged
and a freight train passed

Bad bassist with bow
Pushing furniture around
is what he sounds like

Sty, crick in my neck
zit on the bridge of my nose
and a pizza burn

The oak feels mighty
even as a thin sapling
sinking it's tap root

Teenager'd rather
be a movie star's PA
than a scientist

Sedate all rhinos
and dye their horns magenta
Poachers lose interest

Sign at the mailbox
announces the new baby
A two ballooner!!!

Ninja assassin
treads on the nightingale floor
Freezes and gets set

Pimento stuffer
temporarily shut down
Olive pitter broke

Guy wants Batman mask
Girl does the classic eye roll
Guy hangs it back up

Claire invents the knot
Lived in the reeds by the stream
6000 BC

A ditch full of mud
splattered weeds and an old tire
That's where Steve Snake lives

Dig through a drawer
Toss all the unneeded things
over your shoulder

Instead of chemo
I'm taking a vacation
Nome first, then Fiji

Maternity ward
Midnight, the shift nurse reading
Lovecraft at her desk

Prescription labels
on Elvis' pill bottles
"MAY CAUSE DIZZINESS"

My cube neighbor talks
through the wall about her kids
I play Solitaire

She met him online
Is considering moving
near the jail he's in

The mockingbird mocks
the sound of my maracas
quite well I must say

Magic Lamp recall
Rub one of Lot #5
a fart smell comes out

All my kinfolk love
to dip their soda crackers
in salad dressing

Stalled jigsaw puzzler
wishes there were lightning bolts
in the too much sky

He still wears the shirt
he was shot in years ago
It's brown so looks fine

Act Nineteen: Hobo Cats

Cat's H.A.O.T.
That's "huge amount of trouble"
not N.T.A.A.

Vandals paint the sow
bright blue, farmer tells his son
"Go get the hogwash"

At the beach wedding
sandy wind destroys hairdos
then a squall ruins vows

"How'd you get that scar?"
"Snatched my chain saw from a stump.
Touched it to my nose."

"You look nice today"
"I left my glasses at home"
she said and then sighed

Ave Maria
amazing at the wedding
sung by Joe Cocker

Cats use hobo signs
left behind from the 20's
like Mean Dog Lives Here

The Shadow Hunter
patrols while I sleep at night,
flashlight taped to broom

The huddled herd braced
against bitter snowy wind
with eyes tightly shut

Every Beethoven
manuscript's chicken scratchy
Publisher' won't care

Child draws pentagrams
on the floor with dark crayons
Hears clip clop of hooves

Man chases top hat
Trips over his walking stick
Sprawled, then hat rolls back

My skateboard was safe
Had 4 sets of wheels, not 2
and was Stop sign shaped

Prone to getting lost
New Subaru Meanders
have no GPS

Polka band's van parked
in the Shoney's parking lot
with headlights left on

Grizzly bear standing
on a whale carcass washed up
on the grey sand beach

When you speak to me
you don't make a lot of sense
I really like that

Moth eggs resemble
the yellow Chinese checkers
before the game starts

In my cubicle
a dusty CPR mask
waits on a tack

I

Bees land and enter
the eyes of my Wolfman mask
stored in the tool shed

II

Instantly I start
organizing syllables
while I close the door

I may have latent
cat burglar skills I can use
to get your pearls back

A spider drops down
in front of the camera lens
during Game 7

Stoned at a red light
so, when the lighter pops out
I drive straight on through

Monkeys pick pockets
and use the coins to buy fruit
from the street vendors

Gail wept when assigned
Boulez's Third Sonata
for her recital

I built a treehouse
out of old popsicle sticks
for your ficus tree

Lions lap up coffee
relishing how good it is
after heavy meals

Ringing the doorbell
with a large deep-dish veggie
Hearing the dog bark

Fidgety patient
after chemotherapy
pleading for a smoke

Ted's van is haunted
by the ghost of a bear cub
he hit years ago

Early for AA
Parked in the empty church lot
Sips to go coffee

Hungover carney
flannel shirt moist from the dew
cranks open a ride

I'd worked all Christmas
on an Etch a Sketch Santa
which my sister shook

My neighbors, Blue Cheer
were surprisingly quiet
Turned in early too

I'm startled awake
Dogs barking into the woods
straining their chains taut

Two little girls float
from the shed toward the house
with blank expressions

Long night, no contact
The dawn brightens the pulled shades
So, the sêance ends

Bow a trumpet bell
and if I'm not mistaken
you'll get a B-flat

No birthday candles
so, we lit Dorito shards
An old Boy Scout trick

We don't do bonsai
Our sea onion's been growing
for 40 years though

My swampwise wife says
"Slap your hand on the water
to call that gator"

Spock walks distracted
across Altar IV staring
at his tricorder

Full Moon, toss and turn
Finally get a few hours' sleep
Wake up, stinging eyes

Bad result car wash
Parked it in the rain, then smeared
with paper towels

I was fearless once
I'd take on anything... then
think I'd done it well

To best scare someone
twist the fake snake in your hands
not showing its head

Mom "invents" nachos
while we watch the Moon landing
and becomes legend

My worst fire mistake
was setting a Dixie cup
full of gas ablaze

Rumpled man dresses
like his apartment's a hoard
and his car burns oil

If I were ivy
I wouldn't choke trees I'd climb
nice cast iron fences

The reporter asks
"Are you a hero?" I say
"Darn tootin' I am!"

Remember truckin'?
Well, I'm majorly surprised
Our mailman does it

I pass up crawfish
Too much work per bite plus juice
runs down both arms

My seldom used heart
stored in an old Pennzoil box
with flaps left open

Old sepia print
of a girl in lace possessed
Hands covered in flies

Sunday hangover
with the Monaco Grand Prix
on at full volume

Small burr on the can
I nicked my thumb, got some blood
in my hominy

Blue ribbon orchids
grown at Springbok Farms using
only puzzle dust

There's a bitter spot
Shows up on most x-ray scans
of my healthy heart

Steven Hawking thinks
England should wear red jerseys
to win the World Cup

Forest Service Drone
3 takes some hi-def footage
of a blond sasquatch

Act Twenty: Squirrels Sipping Kool-Aid

Squirrels sipping Kool-Aid
left on the picnic tables
by kids at the swings

Chloe's new dollhouse
trashed by Sebastian the cat
through the open walls

Circus bear rides bikes
Prefers the ones with a bell
which he rings and rings

The stoned farmer plows
thinking more about a maze
than a bumper crop

We're not smart phony
We're old and set in our ways
We're more land liney

RELEASE THE KRACKEN

...AND BETTER WARN KRACKENVILLE
IT'LL HEAD THERE FIRST

DENISE FEEDS THE SWANS
IRANIAN CAVIAR
SHE TOOK FROM THE FRIDGE

THE MILK MAN'S STARTLED
WHEN DELTA WING JETS ROAR BY
LOW OVER OUR STREET

"THE SQUIRREL"
"I BEND A BRANCH DOWN
THEN JUMP TO ANOTHER ONE
BEND THAT ONE DOWN TOO"

AT THE PEZ MUSEUM
THE RARE STALIN DISPENSER
RECEIVES THE MOST SCORN

"WHY AM I DOWN HERE"
THE WINGED CHARIOT DRIVER
SAID "IN ALL THIS DUST"

SOUVENIR DRIFTWOOD
STOLEN OFF OUR DECK BY SQUIRRELS
WHO LOVE THAT SEA SALT

My bug hands and feet
let me climb walls easily
With shoes off of course

Sudokumakers
leave numbers in their gridworld
of easy and hard

At "The Birds" remake
the director misses calls
His ringtone's bird calls

Ancient aliens
wear air-conditioned work suits
at Puma Punku

Car left in the snow
on a road between two hills
Driver's door open

Just relax, be cool
That's a cross goose you're seeing
on Pokemon GO

Stinkpie's now 80
Guy laughs at his name, Stink sighs
Throws another punch

I inherited
my old baby monitor
we thought was haunted

Bird attacks tiger
Swoops in, quick butt peck, swoops out
Tiger's spooked, swats air

I'm the Richard Pryor
of cheese dip, meaning I eat
...until it's all gone

Moonshiner's cow shoes
made their footprints look like hooves
to Revenuers

My best Jell-O mold
makes Portuguese man-o-wars
Lime with cayenne sting

I don't believe it
Our wedding DJ starts off
with AC/DC

My shocking next life
I'm reborn from my wax pod
in a hive of bees

Seven hummingbirds
perched on the feeder feeding
Benihana style

That's some good hot sauce
First bite I coughed, then shuddered,
then got the hiccups

Vampire crepe myrtle
Blood red blooms, leaves so dark green
that they're almost black

The play is ruined
by one open safety pin
in the corpse's cape

Don't get distracted
and hold that pill in your mouth
Pink is NOT cherry

Set an extra place
for the ghost of mean Aunt Mae
who didn't like ham

A dirty white van
unloading a heavy bag
at the mall dumpster

Yellow highlighter
gives a good jaundiced skin tone
for your "I'm sick" post

Me at my window
aiming my toy machine gun
at all passers by

"Did you sleep well, dear?"
"No, ghosts kept pinching my toes"
she said with a limp

We're approached by cops
Steve Smith says, "Give a fake name"
so, I say "Steve Smith"

I don't say "Bless you"
I don't feel I'm qualified
I've got tissues though

I'm gonna leave work,
go home, and start this damn day
all over again

Nature takes over
Chernobyl's bumper car rink
Wolf pups in the cars

Two anxious tankers
think they hear planes approaching
through the snowy sky

Drive Thru Safari
closed since their rhinos have learned
to open car doors

Unflinching jumper
head first off the 10th floor ledge
with hands in pockets

Stolen robot car
returns to its owner's house
with the thief locked in

Men on bull shaped bikes
give the kids a warm up run
before Pamplona

Spell witch with 2 v's
instead of the w
Makes it look boding

Low flying saucer
shiny black with one bright light
tilts to miss treetops

Pepper blog shuts down
The Carolina Reaper
episode went south

Invading army
just wades around the east end
of China's Great Wall

Parmesan nachos
smell like a jigsaw puzzle
on fire in the den

Old cat fakes a limp
Hits upon the perfect way
to get adopted

Chunks of midnight sky
fell on a town in Utah
Some fell down chimneys

"Glassblower Haiku"
You want a freak accident?
...or a lovely vase

"...so, you're good to go,"
he said to the man he was
anxious to have leave

She breaks up with me
again, so I crash and burn
but phoenix next day

Chef has taste nightmares
like soup served in asphalt bowls
or pecan pulp bread

Owls can see through snow
but keep it secret from mice
who dash under it

Elderly drummer
choppy and feeble with sticks
but suave with brushes

I kept my Clackers
and became extremely good
Kept my lawn darts too

Space station panel
falls into the atmosphere
Can't they tighten bolts?

Act Twenty-One: Moonshine Jelly

Bought moonshine jelly
Had cloth wrapped around the lid
Tasted like apple

"Why no new web posts?"
"Our store is being ransacked
and we're held hostage"

Under the trap door
I'm waiting for Houdini
to drop through handcuffed

Submarine ride con
Pay 90 bucks, get sealed in
then they just tilt it

Forgotten popcorn
Pot glows orange, smoke billows out
Cat's under the bed

Shepherd lets his goats
climb trees, they enjoy it so
Shouts "Come down, let's go!"

My cheap ball point pen
Prone to strokes, meaning ink clots
break loose ruining words

Newlywed groceries
Hamburger Helper and a
Gourmet magazine

Cat tiptoe walking
across the top of the fence
as it sprinkles rain

Santa's not got one
but Smoky the Bear sure does
It's his own zip code

Footprints in the snow
getting more and more shallow
as Angel ascends

Hitler had survived
the bomb under the table
toed under too far

"Your parrot say more
than Danger Will Robinson?"
"Nope, that's about it"

Looks like a straight line
but it's just a tiny part
of a huge circle

Ice cream pops these days
Smaller than they use to be
Two small bites then stick

I'm Thomas Pynchon
All this is a new hobby
I'm not good at yet

They play some New Age
first fifteen minutes each day
at rehab clinics

01001
0000110
1001, y'all

An entire oak tree
contained in the orangeish pulp
of one small acorn

He's got an I've been
in trouble but know how to
get out of it smile

Searchsong of the shark
hummed quietly to itself
swimming between meals

I left Dad's best saw
out in the Seattle rain
Now it's rusty dull

Ethical Hacker
position available
Shadyness condoned

Summoned some spirits
with my Ouija board mouse pad
by clicking on Print

My dream catcher
I hang it up but mainly
it just catches dust

Sirens on the road
heard at the Ranger station
Smoke drifts through the trees

In the dark of night
Grandfather clock in the hall
flashed bright by lightning

Park under a tree
Windshield gets small beads of sap
Which your wipers smear

Where the pond once was
there's only muddy puddles
after the earthquake

Bruce Willis comes out
of retirement to rescue
his kidnapped daughter

Interstate advice
Bug splats? Start windshield washer
quick before it dries

"And" is a bit bland,
but "but" adds kick, "if" suspense,
and "umm" confusion

Dancing in the house
Treasured bric-a-brac vibrates
to the edge of shelves

Fight in the mess hall
English peas were being served
and many got crushed

The gargoyle sits bored
on the edge of the building
Chin held in his hands

Want to sneeze real hard?
Wonder what jalapeno
powder might smell like.

Bach jots down a few
atonal chords, then glances
over his shoulder

On a dark Nile night
Cleopatra's pleasure barge
glides by all lit up

My old Oldsmobile
burps into life swallowing
a quart of hi-test

Frightened young zebra
covered in odorous mud
ignored by his mom

Showy sand castle
topped with mixed drink umbrellas
Soon they're all that's left

Smallest potato
boils to the edge of the pot
and almost hops out

Child leaves the campsite
wanders off into the dark
lured by clicking sounds

1/1/2000
No planes fell, no missiles fired,
no canned food needed

The mind reader's shaken
He'd confirmed life after death
when his subject died

The Jumbotron truck
has been delayed in traffic
The remote truck too

The log rolling team
stays at the new Ramada
built where woods were cleared

Parents named him Georj
Georj had to explain that j
the rest of his life

We taped and played back
Revolution No. 9
backwards, got stoned first

We built our snowman
in the graveyard where the snow's
velvety and still

I'm not a rebel
without a cause, I've got one
It's just a dumb cause

I

A small tornado
crosses the four lane right in front
of my hapless van

II

So, I bounced across
the median, headed home,
called in sick to work

If you need to point
at Disneyland they train you
to use 2 fingers

Yes, I am psychic
That's how I became famous
metal detecting

Only clam chowder
left behind on the soup aisle
before Katrina

One hospital charged
new Moms to hold their babies
$39

Astronaut wants tea
Wonders can you steep in space?
And what if you stir

Canaries float by
their well-built cage now a boat
with plenty of seeds

Placed the needle down
on my first Stones 45
"crack pop crack pop pop"

The hurricane comes
Colonials near the coast
are so ill prepared

Throwing arms wide, yells
"Nature's GREAT", hits his wife's head
with his hiking stick

Act Twenty-Two: Bear-Made Hammocks

Bears make hammocks now
They're crude and don't swing so well
Lumberjacks find them

Book soaked in spilled booze
Dry for years now I'm sober
Love to flip through it

Huge Gettysburg oak
pulls up some Civil War loot
when it's blown over

Cartoons ain't real life
When you start to run away
you don't hear bongos

The ant doesn't know
it's being watched from above
and I'm so benign

My robotic hands
snap KitKats in two better
than my old flesh ones

Spent jack-o-lantern
goes soft on the compost heap
Eyes once lit now dark

Grandkid snuggles up
to Grandpa who's been snacking
"You smell like Fritos"

Scout and Jem were wrong
Boo Radley ate Spam, not cats
It just smells like cats

The weasel goes POP
The monkey pulls back startled
Mulberries fall off

The new nanodrones
can hover in a keyhole
while reconing rooms

Things happen to trees
in deep woods you just don't know
Things that topple them

Our new fire station
has no pole which disappoints
all the old-timers

Best wild drum solos
include a little cowbell
Just a few tinkles

I catch tiny sprites
who in the Mason jar look
like blue lightning bugs

My Japanese wife
keeps caged crickets in each room
I dread getting home

First time out hiking
Haikus came like falling leaves
Next time, sore back, zilch

Their written language
All U's with just the slightest
variation each

Walked like a chicken
for days after lifting out
that Jeep transmission

Bird spills tobacco
from a stolen meerschaum pipe
all over my car

COME SEE GATORLAND
Left on State Road 6, Snow Cones
& Ample Parking

Don't fact check me so
It's Google Google Google
everything I say

Dog's anti-itch cone
fills up with snow while he's out
doing his business

A make-do planet
now within reach by spaceships
from our worn-out Earth

Extreme comb-overs
the Japanese call "barcodes"
Dewy ground "roji"

"The Optimist (?)"
The glass is half full
Yes, but it's lukewarm Coke
ice has melted in

After a few drinks
6 and 7 letter words
get replaced by 4

First patters of rain
on our tent lulls us to sleep
in the dry ravine

Don't help the software
It will edit forms just fine
all by by itself

Ill man in a pew
lit by one concentrated
beam of cleansing light

Split biscuits in half
Sop syrup with the bottoms
Spread jam on the tops

Weak Georgia earthquake
sounds like our washing machine
came on a second

Crashed my toy airplane
into our station wagon
Left a nose sized dent

Keith Moon often took
buffalo tranquilizer
to steady tempos

Found some sunglasses
worth like $200
They're wraparounds, scratched

Russian rocket train
could do 300 easy
but took off on curves

Her life's all messed up
but she sure can style your hair
and talk the whole time

The best new advance
in Mars Rover design
is the serpent shape

With my Hershey's Kiss
I got a small piece of foil
Tasted like tinsel

Mary Todd was miffed
Lincoln slept on the sofa
Woke with a stiff neck

The intrepid pig
squeezes through the narrow gap
between rose hedges

She opens the door
and THERE's the cactus monster
with its spiny hands

My pet goat Luther
narrows his eyes playing up
looking like Satan

Campbell on the slant
Snags pass thirty twenty ten
Touchdown!! Earl Campbell

Jetsam on the beach
plus, a gigantic whale skull
cracked from ramming ships

My staring at Fran
affects her nervous system
enough to glance back

A meteor falls
while a volcano erupts
Sure fire three-point shot

A Potato Moon
when it has a brownish hue
and viewed from Boise

Paul Bunyan picks up
a school bus full of children
stuck in a snowbank

Some tortoise hatchlings
gather around a pansy
and gobble it up

Combine a hammock
with a zip line and your naps
never get started

The Saint Bernard found
ski poles in the fresh powder
but no one around

The undertaker
is sloppy with nail polish
and only has red

Surprisingly fun
Smear Elmer's glue on your palm
Let it dry, then peel

Hugh island of trash
in the Indian Ocean
with plastic bag beach

"If you murder me
don't take a polygraph test"
She said, lovingly

Got shocked by canned goods
rolling my rickety cart
through Piggly Wiggly

Touch hammer to nail
Just a short little love tap
before the drama

The circus owner
has a private trampoline
for his kangaroo

Instead of a tip
Picasso left a doodle
for his stressed waiter

Bitter Park needs work
The monkey bars are rusty
plus, there's copperheads

Act Twenty-Three: Click Restart

The ordinance crew
paint the armored bulldozer
pink with green blotches

An older Tom Cruise
signs on to play Rasputin
"I get the girl, right?"

I fell back in bed
Banged my head on the headboard
Saw a flash of light

Screen froze, clicked Restart
Brief image of the Devil
Then it went Blue Screen

My band the Pell-Mells
does a lot of old timey
Hong Kong surf music

The preacher chain smokes
the night before his sermon
about temptation

Women with beehives
leave the Tupperware party
in their flying cars

Old out of sorts cat
Calico, with huge vet bills
must be truly loved

I run the machine
that clamps the metal nose weights
on balsa wood planes

Mule steps on a tack
and for the rest of the day
goes click clop clop clop

Ray punched through storm clouds
Lit our path down the steep slope
while all else was dark

Deft birds make twig roofs
over abandoned Fall nests
for cold snowy nights

My Christmas sweater
with Bigfoot dressed as Santa
won the Most Tacky

I spotted Mothman
hovering above our barn
sipping a juice box

My great grandfather
was the first to wear lampshades
at parties, wakes too

Cat jumps off the fridge
Beautiful arc, paws outstretched
Firm thump, then slight limp

My king is in check
so, I castle, suggesting
him running inside

Sleepy on I-10
Closed my eyes for just a sec
Woke up upside down

Kid hovers over
a big bin of gummi worms
'til no one's looking

Bob Dylan backstage
at the Nobel Prize show
wishing he'd gone on

Snow and fog combine
to cloak both the ground and air
in cigar smoke white

A row of blackbirds
perched on a telegraph wire
watch two fight midair

Granny does wheelies
on her bike with a basket
to impress the kids

Albino raccoon
missing the black bandit mask
still steals the cat food

Lucifer has dreams
the first ones in centuries
of snow covered hills

Bass drum still strapped on
he quits the parade dizzy
and sits on a bench

The elder Matisse
ties a brush to a long stick
and paints sitting down

Brian Jones sliced up
speaker cones to get his sound
for Satisfaction

Old man confesses
"There's a body in the well
we've barely used since"

It's either the world's
gotten more slippery, or
I'm less sure footed

Loose words swept by wind
waft away... but some break free
and gibber the ground

Guillotine lackey
tasked with replacing baskets
about once a week

Frog throws up an arm
and goes "Yee haaaa !!!" while riding
a rhino beetle

Wyatt Earp saucers
his coffee so it'll cool
and not burn his mouth

She sprinkles pepper
on her platter of French fries
Really goes to town

One little paw print
in the rolled-out pizza dough
while my back was turned

Roosters love hot sauce
Not universally known
but they lap it up

The grouchy woman
Grouchy because her new boots
are Barbie feet shaped

Death bed arsonist
wants a Viking funeral
Makes his wife promise

To my British friend
"That'll knock you a-winding"
Him "What's a-winding?"

Stole slips off hanger
Ends up on the closet floor
kicked behind the shoes

Cat tries to help bake
but just ends up swatting flour
all over the place

"The Makapansgat Pebble"
I found a cool rock
and took it back to my cave
3,000,000 BC

Robots report back
"There's a pulsating bubble
in Fukushima"

Through the old dog door
comes the possum that visits
my great aunt Sadie

Bees make blue honey
in Mississippi with dye
from the Levi plant

The peerless goat jumps
from one cliff to another
Seems to hang mid air

Madge Lamborghini
has heard every car comeback
that can be cameback

Two geese flying low
arguing in loud sharp honks
flap land on the green

Roll a bowling ball
across bubble wrap pop. pop..
pop... pop... pop..... pop...... pop.......

Georgia O'Keefe said
"I've painted those hills so much
God gave them to me"

For our phoneless kids
I've hung 12 wind chimes inside
our car for long trips

The stray cat dozing
on our butcher shop awning
waits for some trimmed fat

I have several heads
to use for job interviews
all with the same grin

Robbie the Robot
now retired heats up some oil
in his double wide

Andy Warhol buys
Brillo pads on Aisle 7
but just needs the box

Teddy Roosevelt
rides a moose across a lake
Secret Service, cow

Otters juggle stones
most times laying on their backs
and when they're alone

The pesky parrot
resists being hypnotized
Goes "AWWWK", "awww", then "aw..."

Japanese soldiers
left for years on Mindoro
watch cruise ships pass by

James Joyce is banished
to the tool shed by his wife
when he smokes his pipe

German tabby cat
picks up a few English words
from Baywatch reruns

Fisher and Spassky
Who killed those 2 flies? And why.
Not radiation

Shallow back yard lake
Rain water caught by a pool
that use to be there

If you let us put
SEE ROCK CITY on your barn
we'll paint it for free

Says "Lord have mercy"
about once every minute
reading the paper

I'm throwing away
that expired Merthiolate
It's got mercury

I

Free jazz group starts with
"Ah, Sweet Mystery of Life"
as a slowed down dirge

II

Then they take flight with
"Take the A Train" in three four
like Sun Ra did it

Cool guy at Parkview
in bed getting oxygen
with sunglasses on

When I get things right
Boom chahka lahka lahka's
what I saw, calmly

If you're reading this
Thanks so much for being here
or you've jumped ahead

ABOUT THE AUTHOR

Billy Traylor grew up in LaGrange, a small town in Georgia. He studied music and played in regional orchestras before taking up haiku writing.

Made in the USA
Columbia, SC
08 April 2018